REVIEWS OF NATIONAL POLICIES FOR EDUCATION

DENMARK
Educating Youth

ORGANISATION FOR ECONOMIC CO-OPERATION AND DEVELOPMENT

ORGANISATION FOR ECONOMIC CO-OPERATION AND DEVELOPMENT

Pursuant to Article 1 of the Convention signed in Paris on 14th December 1960, and which came into force on 30th September 1961, the Organisation for Economic Co-operation and Development (OECD) shall promote policies designed:

- to achieve the highest sustainable economic growth and employment and a rising standard of living in Member countries, while maintaining financial stability, and thus to contribute to the development of the world economy;
- to contribute to sound economic expansion in Member as well as non-member countries in the process of economic development; and
- to contribute to the expansion of world trade on a multilateral, non-discriminatory basis in accordance with international obligations.

The original Member countries of the OECD are Austria, Belgium, Canada, Denmark, France, Germany, Greece, Iceland, Ireland, Italy, Luxembourg, the Netherlands, Norway, Portugal, Spain, Sweden, Switzerland, Turkey, the United Kingdom and the United States. The following countries became Members subsequently through accession at the dates indicated hereafter: Japan (28th April 1964), Finland (28th January 1969), Australia (7th June 1971), New Zealand (29th May 1973) and Mexico (18th May 1994). The Commission of the European Communities takes part in the work of the OECD (Article 13 of the OECD Convention).

370
.9489
D397a

Publié en français sous le titre :
EXAMENS DES POLITIQUES NATIONALES D'ÉDUCATION
DANEMARK
La formation des jeunes

© OECD 1995
Applications for permission to reproduce or translate all or part
of this publication should be made to:
Head of Publications Service, OECD
2, rue André-Pascal, 75775 PARIS CEDEX 16, France

FOREWORD

The first *OECD Reviews of National Policies for Education in Denmark* (1980) was based on a national prospective report on education in 1990 and addressed the entire education system.

This report deals with youth education and the problems posed by its reform. It is divided in two parts: a summary of the Background Report* prepared for the review by the Danish authorities, and the OECD Examiners' Report.

The examiners were Mr. Bolton (United Kingdom), Mr. Brenner (Germany), Mr. Feldt (Sweden) and Mr. van Vught (the Netherlands).

This volume is published on the responsibility of the Secretary-General of the OECD.

* The complete Background Report is available from:
Danish Ministry of Education
Undervisningsministeriets forlag,
Frederiksholms Kanal 25 F,
DK-1220 Copenhagen K.
Tel.: +45 33 92 5220

TABLE OF CONTENTS

The OECD Examiners and the Danish Delegation 7

Part One
YOUTH EDUCATION IN DENMARK
PROBLEMS AND ACHIEVEMENTS
Summary of the Background Report

Chapter 1
The Kingdom of Denmark — A Short Presentation

Geography	11
History	12
The Labour Market and the Work Force	12
The Danish Economy	13
Denmark's Parliament and Government	17

Chapter 2
Presentation of the Danish Educational System

The Municipal School (*Folkeskolen*)	21
The *Gymnasium* in its Present Form	24
Vocational Education and Training	25
Post-secondary and Higher Education	25
Adult Education and Training	26
The Danish Marking System	26

Chapter 3
The Development during the Last Decade

Education and the Labour Market	31
New Mechanisms of Funding — The "Taximeter" System	32
The State Education Grant and Loan Scheme	33
Decentralisation of the Steering of the Programmes of Education	34
Increased Decentralisation and Institutional Self-regulation	34
The Project on Content and Quality Development	35
The Costs of Education	36
Choices and Networks — New Concepts in Education	39
Internationalisation of Danish Education	41
Reference	43

5

Chapter 4
Youth Education

Vocationally Oriented Education	45
Upper Secondary Education	64
Alternative and Supplementary Education and Training for the 14-18-Year-Olds	78

Chapter 5
Problems and Challenges

The Drop-out Problem of Youth Education	83
The Act on Vocational Basic Course — EGU	85
The Action Plan "Education for All"	85
Adult Education	89
Credit Transfer	89

Part Two
EXAMINERS' REPORT

Chapter 1
Introduction

Chapter 2
Remit and Issues

Chapter 3
Transversal Themes

Employment and the Labour Market	99
Distribution of Policy and Financial Authority	102
Quality and Standards	103
Student Drop-out	106

Chapter 4
Youth Education

Vocational Education and Training (VET)	110
The *Gymnasium*	115
Other Youth Education	117

Chapter 5
Before and After

The *Folkeskole*	119
Higher Education	120

Chapter 6
Conclusions and Recommendations

Conclusions	123
Recommendations	124

THE OECD EXAMINERS

Mr. Eric BOLTON	Rapporteur, the Institute of Education, University of London, Former head of Her Majesty's Inspectorate in England, United Kingdom
Mr. Karsten BRENNER	Ministerialdirigent, Bundesministeriium für Bildung und Wissenschaft, Germany
Mr. Kjell-Olof FELDT	Former Minister of Finance, Sweden
Mr. Frans A. VAN VUGHT	Director of the Centre for Higher Education Policy Studies, University of Twente, the Netherlands

THE DANISH DELEGATION

Mr. Ole Vig JENSEN	Minister for Education
Ms. Inge THYGESEN	Permanent Secretary
Mr. Ernst GOLDSCHMIDT	Senior Advisor
Ms. Hanna DAM	Under-Secretary
Ms. Berrit HANSEN	Director-General
Mr. Niels HUMMELUHR	Director-General
Mr. Sten GRAMBYE	Director-General
Mr. Holger KNUDSEN	Director-General
Mr. Uffe Gravers PEDERSEN	Director-General
Mr. Torben Kornbech RASMUSSEN	Director-General
Mr. Kim Mørch JACOBSEN	Director-General
Mr. Roland ØSTERLUND	Head of Division
Ms. Bodil Mørkøv ULLERUP	Private Secretary to the Minister
Ms. Eli BIKER	Head of Section
Ms. Marilou PEHRSON	Secretary

Permanent Delegation of Denmark to the OECD

Mr. T. MAILAND CHRISTENSEN   Ambassador - Permanent Representative

Mr. Arne HAUGE JENSEN   Secretary of Embassy

Part One

**YOUTH EDUCATION IN DENMARK
PROBLEMS AND ACHIEVEMENTS**

Summary of the Background Report

Chapter 1

THE KINGDOM OF DENMARK — A SHORT PRESENTATION

Geography

Denmark covers 43 000 km² consisting of the peninsula Jutland (30 000 km²) and 483 islands (13 000 km²) of which 97 are inhabited. The biggest islands are Zealand with the capital, Copenhagen, Funen and Lolland-Falster. Denmark is a lowland — the highest point is only 184 meter — with a temperate coastal climate.

The number of inhabitants is 5.13 million. In relation to Denmark's continental neighbours the population density is moderate (119 inh./km²) but high compared with the rest of the Nordic countries (13-18 inh./km²). From Table 1 it can be seen that the population density varies pretty much.

Table 1. **Main provinces of Denmark with respect to area, population and population density**

	Area (%)	Population (%)	Density (inhabitants/km²)
Jutland	69	46	79
Zealand*	17	42	289
Funen	8	9	130
Other islands	6	3	71
Total	100	100	119

* With the capital metropolitan area.
Source: Danish Ministry of Education (1994), *Danish Youth Education, Problems and Achievements*.

The local Danish administration is divided into 275 municipalities — varying in size from 4 000 to 550 000 inhabitants — and 14 counties plus the City of Copenhagen and Frederiksberg.

The Danish Kingdom also comprises the two self-governing territories, the Faroe Islands in the Atlantic (1 400 km² and 48 000 inhabitants) and Greenland (2 175 million km² and 56 000 inhabitants). The Faroe Islands and Greenland are, however, not dealt with in this report, as education falls within the competence of the legislatures and the governments of the two territories.

Denmark is — and has always been — a European crossroad. Denmark forms a bridge between Scandinavia and Central Europe and is at the same time the gateway between the Baltic Sea region and the rest of the world. The Danish straits, the Sound and the Great Belt are some of the most busy in the world.

History

Denmark is a very old kingdom. The first names of Danish kings are found in historical sources from the 9th century, when they fought against the German-Roman emperors.

During the Viking Age and the Middle Ages Denmark was an expansive power. A power which reached its height in 1397 when a personal union, "The Kalmar Union" gathered Denmark, Norway and Sweden with Finland under the Danish crown in order to resist the Hanseatic League and the German-Roman Empire. The Swedes, however, getting more and more dissatisfied with the Union's Danish dominance, broke out in the beginning of the 16th century. During the next two centuries frequent Danish-Swedish wars were fought for the command of the Baltic Sea region. Denmark finally lost the struggle and its old eastern provinces Scania, Blekinge and Halland at the southern tip of the Scandinavian peninsula. Norway remained in the union until 1814, when it was forced into a new union with Sweden as one of the costs of Denmark/Norway's alliance with Napoleon. After a war in 1864 Denmark lost Schleswig-Holstein to Prussia. After the first World War and a referendum in 1920 the northern part of Schleswig, however, came back to Denmark.

The outcome of "the decline and fall of the Danish empire" is a country with a very homogeneous population with its own national language. This homogeneity has promoted the endeavours to make compromises and reach consensus which characterises the Danish society and makes it comparatively stable and well organised.

The Danish laws on general and local elections are based upon the principle of proportional representation. No political party has therefore had the absolute majority in the Parliament and very seldom in a local council for the last century. As a consequence the governments have always been coalition-governments or minority governments dependent upon co-operation and compromises with other parties.

The Labour Market and the Work Force

The Danish labour market is regarded as stable and well organised. The percentage of employees and employers who are members of unions and employers' organisations respectively is high and collective bargaining takes place within a framework of fixed precepts. After a very long strike and lockout in 1899 the unions and the employers' organisations made a general agreement, "the September agreement" or "the Constitution of the Labour market". According to this agreement, which was last revised in 1986, notified strikes and lockouts were acknowledged, and the workers recognized the employer's right to direct and allocate the work. Furthermore the "September agreement" enjoined both parties an embargo on striking and lockouts as long as a collective agreement was in force — normally two years — and set rules for the fixing of dead-line for the denunciation of collective agreements.

In order to support the two parties' efforts to create orderly conditions on the labour market two acts on the establishment of a conciliation institution and a Labour Court were passed in 1910 with the last revisions in 1971 and 1973.

Table 2 shows the economically active part of the Danish population divided into age groups, sexes and level of education.

It appears from the table that the level of education of the labour force is rising significantly: 67.1 per cent of the 55-64-year-olds have only had seven years of compulsory education, while the percentage of 25-39-year-olds with no other formal education than compulsory education is down to 26.3 per cent. It should also be noted that a high percentage of the women (72.4 per cent) — like in the other Nordic countries — are economically active on the labour market.

Like in most European countries the level of unemployment in Denmark is high — 12.1 on 1 December 1993. Table 3 shows that those with no other formal education than compulsory education and women are most strongly affected. But the table also shows that unemployment is a serious problem at all levels of education.

The Danish Economy

The Danish GDP amounted to 694.5 billion DKr (91.9 billion ECU) in 1990 or 134 529 DKr (17 795 ECU) per inhabitant.

Denmark has always been lacking in raw-materials until the very last years, when the exploitation of the oil and gasfields in the Danish sector of the North Sea has made Denmark selfsupplying with liquid fuel. Danish industry and agriculture are therefore very dependent on import of raw materials and semi-manufactured goods. Consequently the business life of Denmark has always been very dependent on a high rate of export. The value of Danish foreign trade (import and export) per inhabitant (79 775 DKr, or 10 552 ECU, in 1990) is one of the highest in the world.

Until the 1960s agricultural products accounted for the main part of Danish export, but since then industrial products have taken the lead, for the time being accounting for approximately 60 per cent of the total export. Nevertheless agriculture, which only employs 7 per cent of the workforce, accounts for more than 1/3 of the total export corresponding to 2/3 of its production.

Table 2. Economically active population by age, sex and level of education, 1991

TOTAL M + F	Compulsory education	Upper sec. educ./gen.	Upper sec. educ./voc.	Higher education Short-cycle	Higher education Medium-cycle	Higher educ. university final degree	Total
16-19	88 828	35 094	54 005	1	7	0	177 935
per cent	49.9	19.7	30.4	0.0	0.0	0.0	100.0
20-24	39 528	56 445	154 403	2 535	6 400	553	259 864
per cent	15.2	21.7	59.4	1.0	2.5	0.2	100.0
25-39	210 215	60 061	432 286	38 198	132 050	44 369	918 979
per cent	23.1	6.5	47.0	4.2	14.4	4.8	100.0
40-54	433 678	10 366	259 264	25 258	114 852	39 846	883 264
per cent	49.1	1.2	29.4	2.9	13.0	4.5	100.0
55-64	159 778	634	61 909	4 594	23 757	9 048	259 720
per cent	61.5	0.2	23.8	1.8	9.1	3.5	100.0
65-69	28 267	77	7 576	658	2 700	2 579	41 857
per cent	67.5	0.2	18.1	1.6	6.5	6.2	100.0
70 and plus	3 944	5	1 005	91	246	332	5 623
per cent	70.1	0.1	17.9	1.6	4.4	5.9	100.0
Total	**966 038**	**162 682**	**970 448**	**71 335**	**280 012**	**96 727**	**2 547 242**
per cent	**37.9**	**6.4**	**38.1**	**2.8**	**11.0**	**3.8**	**100.0**

Table 2. **Economically active population by age, sex and level of education, 1991** *(cont.)*

MALES	Compulsory education	Upper sec. educ./gen.	Upper sec. educ./voc.	Higher education Short-cycle	Higher education Medium-cycle	Higher educ. university final degree	Total
16-19	53 241	13 760	29 623	0	5	0	96 629
per cent	55.1	14.2	30.7	0.0	0.0	0.0	100.0
20-24	25 670	22 660	86 516	1 502	3 143	342	139 833
per cent	18.4	16.2	61.9	1.1	2.2	0.2	100.0
25-39	109 447	30 305	247 243	21 346	50 031	28 633	487 005
per cent	22.5	6.2	50.8	4.4	10.3	5.9	100.0
40-54	222 785	6 143	140 844	16 768	50 938	28 464	465 942
per cent	47.8	1.3	30.2	3.6	10.9	6.1	100.0
55-64	90 723	284	37 939	3 544	11 593	7 567	151 650
per cent	59.8	0.2	25.0	2.3	7.6	5.0	100.0
65-69	19 455	40	5 251	517	1 701	2 274	29 238
per cent	66.5	0.1	18.0	1.8	5.8	7.8	100.0
70 and plus	2 901	0	739	70	165	290	4 165
per cent	69.7	0.0	17.7	1.7	4.0	7.0	100.0
Total	**524 222**	**73 192**	**548 155**	**43 747**	**117 576**	**67 570**	**1 374 462**
per cent	**38.1**	**5.3**	**39.9**	**3.2**	**8.6**	**4.9**	**100.0**

Table 2. **Economically active population by age, sex and level of education, 1991** *(cont.)*

FEMALES	Compulsory education	Upper sec. educ./gen.	Upper sec. educ./voc.	Higher education Short-cycle	Higher education Medium-cycle	Higher educ. university final degree	Total
16-19	35 587	21 334	24 382	1	2	0	81 306
per cent	43.8	26.2	30.0	0.0	0.0	0.0	100.0
20-24	13 858	33 785	67 887	1 033	3 257	211	120 031
per cent	11.5	28.1	56.6	0.9	2.7	0.2	100.0
25-39	102 568	29 756	185 043	16 852	82 019	15 736	431 974
per cent	23.7	6.9	42.8	3.9	19.0	3.6	100.0
40-54	210 893	4 223	118 420	8 490	63 914	11 382	417 322
per cent	50.5	1.0	28.4	2.0	15.3	2.7	100.0
55-64	69 055	350	23 970	1 050	12 164	1 481	108 070
per cent	63.9	0.3	22.2	1.0	11.3	1.4	100.0
65-69	8 812	37	2 325	141	999	305	12 619
per cent	69.8	0.3	18.4	1.1	7.9	2.4	100.0
70 and plus	1 396	1	44	2	16	6	1 465
per cent	95.3	0.1	3.0	0.1	1.1	0.4	100.0
Total	**441 816**	**89 490**	**422 293**	**27 588**	**162 436**	**29 157**	**1 172 780**
per cent	**37.7**	**7.6**	**36.0**	**2.4**	**13.9**	**2.5**	**100.0**

Source: Danish Ministry of Education (1994), *Danish Youth Education, Problems and Achievements*.

Danish industry consists mainly of small and medium sized enterprises with a few specialised high-tech companies. Thanks to a widespread use of modern technology and a well-educated workforce Danish industry is, however, able to export quality products at competitive prices.

Finally a remarkable growth in the export of services has been seen during the last couple of years.

Denmark's Parliament and Government

The Parliament — *Folketinget* — consists of one chamber with 179 members of which two represent the Faroe Islands and two represent Greenland. After the last general election in 1990 the following eight political parties are represented in the Parliament:

The Social Democratic Party	71 members*
The Conservative People's Party	30 members
Denmark's Liberal Party	30 members**
The Socialists' People's Party	15 members
The Progress Party	12 members
The Centre Democrats	9 members
The Radical Party	7 members
The Christian People's Party	4 members
Independent (elected at the Faroe Islands)	1 member

In January 1993 the Conservative/Liberal minority-government resigned, and was replaced by a majority government based upon the Social Democratic Party, The Radical Party, The Centre Democrats and The Christian People's Party.

As mentioned previously, minority governments are more the rule than the exception in Denmark, and this fact has created a special ability for co-operation and compromises. This ability finds *inter alia* expression in the legislative work in the field of education. The new Act on the *Folkeskole* was thus adopted by seven of the eight parties represented in the Parliament. In the same way the new Act on Basic Vocational Education (EGU) was also adopted by seven parties.

---

*   including one member elected in Greenland and one member elected on the Faroe Islands.
** including one member elected in Greenland.

Table 3. **Unemployed, redundancy, paid and social security clients by age, sex and level of education, November 1991**

TOTAL M + F	Compulsory education	Upper sec. educ./gen.	Upper sec. educ./voc.	Higher education Short-cycle	Higher education Medium-cycle	Higher educ. university final degree	Total
16-19	72 008	25 073	18 340	1	6	0	115 428
per cent	62.4	21.7	15.9	0.0	0.0	0.0	100.0
20-24	34 720	35 412	43 452	851	3 471	276	118 182
per cent	29.4	30.0	36.8	0.7	2.9	0.2	100.0
25-39	119 756	23 641	78 505	4 903	13 565	5 383	245 753
per cent	48.7	9.6	31.9	2.0	5.5	2.2	100.0
40-54	139 385	3 384	40 688	2 673	8 235	2 695	197 060
per cent	70.7	1.7	20.6	1.4	4.2	1.4	100.0
55-64	182 015	464	43 800	1 889	9 403	1 525	239 096
per cent	76.1	0.2	18.3	0.8	3.9	0.6	100.0
Total	547 884	87 974	224 785	10 317	34 680	9 879	915 519
per cent	59.8	9.6	24.6	1.1	3.8	1.1	100.0

Table 3. **Unemployed, redundancy, paid and social security clients by age, sex and level of education, November 1991** *(cont)*

MALES	Compulsory education	Upper sec. educ./gen.	Upper sec. educ./voc.	Higher education Short-cycle	Higher education Medium-cycle	Higher educ. university final degree	Total
16-19	34 236	10 290	8 451	1	3	0	52 981
per cent	64.6	19.4	16.0	0.0	0.0	0.0	100.0
20-24	16 483	14 044	21 094	489	1 918	140	54 168
per cent	30.4	25.9	38.9	0.9	3.5	0.3	100.0
25-39	53 769	10 220	35 286	2 118	5 288	2 919	109 600
per cent	49.1	9.3	32.2	1.9	4.8	2.7	100.0
40-54	53 981	1 832	19 330	1 455	3 187	1 660	81 445
per cent	66.3	2.2	23.7	1.8	3.9	2.0	100.0
55-64	64 785	178	20 761	1 164	3 178	1 071	91 137
per cent	71.1	0.2	22.8	1.3	3.5	1.2	100.0
Total	**223 254**	**36 564**	**104 922**	**5 227**	**13 574**	**5 790**	**389 331**
per cent	**57.3**	**9.4**	**26.9**	**1.3**	**3.5**	**1.5**	**100.0**

Table 3. **Unemployed, redundancy, paid and social security clients by age, sex and level of education, November 1991** *(cont)*

FEMALES	Compulsory education	Upper sec. educ./gen.	Upper sec. educ./voc.	Higher education Short-cycle	Higher education Medium-cycle	Higher educ. university final degree	Total
16-19	37 772	14 783	9 889	0	3	0	62 447
per cent	60.5	23.7	15.8	0.0	0.0	0.0	100.0
20-24	18 237	21 368	22 358	362	1 553	136	64 014
per cent	28.5	33.4	34.9	0.6	2.4	0.2	100.0
25-39	65 987	13 421	43 219	2 785	8 277	2 464	136 153
per cent	48.5	9.9	31.7	2.0	6.1	1.8	100.0
40-54	85 404	1 552	21 358	1 218	5 048	1 035	115 615
per cent	73.9	1.3	18.5	1.1	4.4	0.9	100.0
55-64	117 230	286	23 039	725	6 225	454	147 959
per cent	79.2	0.2	15.6	0.5	4.2	0.3	100.0
Total	**324 841**	**51 478**	**119 964**	**5 094**	**21 119**	**4 092**	**526 588**
per cent	**64.0**	**9.5**	**21.4**	**0.9**	**3.6**	**0.6**	**100.0**

Source: Danish Ministry of Education (1994), *Danish Youth Education, Problems and Achievements*.

Chapter 2

PRESENTATION OF THE DANISH EDUCATIONAL SYSTEM

During the 12th and 13th centuries, grammar schools were established in connection with the Danish cathedrals, and from the beginning of the 15th century the guilds established an apprenticeship system. In 1479 King Christian I got the Pope's permission to establish the University of Copenhagen. This university was for nearly 400 years the only Danish institution of higher education, but during the 19th century a number of specialised institutions were established, *inter alia* Denmark's Technical University, the Royal Veterinary and Agricultural University, the Royal Dental College and the Royal Danish School of Pharmacy.

Generally speaking, one could say that the 19th century was the period where the institutional pattern of Danish education was formed. Seven years of compulsory education — not to be confused with compulsory school attendance — was introduced in 1814 and a system of municipal education authorities was built up, the grammar schools with their classic-linguistic curriculum got a mathematical-scientific branch, and commercial and technical schools and teacher training colleges were established. In addition to this folk high-schools, continuation schools and — as an alternative to the municipal schools — free schools grew up as a result of the popular revival, that characterises this century.

The Municipal School *(Folkeskolen)*

After an extension of compulsory education from 7 to 9 years (7-16 years of age) in 1971 the present Act on the Municipal School — *Folkeskolen* — was adopted in 1975.

The aim of the act was to create equal educational opportunities for all pupils, and the result was the introduction of nine years of comprehensive primary and lower secondary education, combined with a supplementary optional tenth year and an optional preschool class.

The spectrum of school subjects is very broad, and there is a wide range of optional subjects, especially in the last three forms. The curriculum includes a number of practical subjects to enable more practically-minded pupils to develop their interests and abilities.

The school year normally comprises 200 school days. The number of pupils in a normal class must not exceed 28, and the average is 18.

Examinations

The Act introduced a new examination system which may be described as follows:
- there is no overall examination; leaving examinations may be taken on a single-subject basis;
- there are only two examination levels. In the large majority of examination subjects, there is in fact only one examination level;
- it is the pupils themselves who decide whether they want to present themselves for an examination in a particular subject; and
- there is no pass mark.

Pursuant to the Act, the Leaving Examination of the *Folkeskole* (LE) may be taken in eleven subjects, and the Minister is empowered to increase the range of examination subjects to include "other subjects of a practical nature". In certain subjects, the examination may be taken more than once, see table below; this enables a pupil to improve his/her examination results the subsequent year.

The Advanced Leaving Examination of the *Folkeskole* (ALE) may only be taken in five subjects and only at the end of the 10th form. However, in the subjects where both course levels are offered, only the pupils who have followed the advanced course may sit for this examination (with the exception of Danish).

Leaving examinations

Subject	8th	9th	10th
Danish		LE	LE/ALE
Arithmetic/Mathematics		LE	LE/ALE advanced
English		LE	LE/ALE course
Physics/Chemistry		LE	LE/ALE
German		LE	LE/ALE
Latin			LE
French			LE
Creative Art	LE	LE	LE
Woodwork	LE	LE	LE
Home Economics	LE	LE	LE
Typing	LE	LE	LE

On completion of compulsory education, various types of education are open to pupils, for example:

1. General upper secondary education
   a. The *Gymnasium*
   b. The Higher Preparatory Examination (HF) courses

2. Vocational education and training
   a. Basic vocational education and training
   b. Technical and commercial examination courses
   c. Social and health education courses
   d. Other types of vocational education

The new Act on the Folkeskole

In June 1993 the *Folketing* passed a new Act on the *Folkeskole*, which came into force on 1 August 1994.

The act is the third and last stage in an extensive reform of both the government and content of the *Folkeskole*, and is the result of profound discussions among the parties in the Education Committee of Parliament and consultations between the Committee and the Minister for more than a year. An essential part of the basis of the new act was created by a 4-year Innovation Programme for the *Folkeskole*.

The objectives of the *Folkeskole* will basically build upon the objectives of the old act. The crucial innovation is found in the organisation of the teaching content and in the improvement of the methods used for the evaluation of the pupils' benefit and the effect of teaching. Another innovation is the provision that teaching individual subjects shall interact with teaching interdisciplinary topics and problems.

A new subject named "Nature and Technology" is introduced in the 1st-6th form. The teaching of English will begin in the 4th form instead of the 5th, and the provision on the second foreign language promotes a development where French becomes an equal alternative to German.

The existing division of the subjects arithmetic/mathematics, English, German and Physics/Chemistry in basic and advanced courses in the 8th-10th form will be abolished. Instead the new act requests the schools and the teachers to adapt teaching to the qualifications of the individual pupils. This has to be done on the basis of a running internal evaluation and fixing of goals for the individual pupil and groups of pupils. In order to vary the evaluation of the pupils' benefit of their schooling a mandatory project assignment will be fixed by a ministerial order, but the topic of the project will be chosen totally by the schools and the teachers (see Figure 1).

The existing leaving examinations at the end of the 8th and 10th forms will be maintained, but the requirements at the 9th form examination (LE) will become more vigorous.

When the new curricula and syllabuses are developed it should also be taken into consideration that the minimum number of weekly lessons has been increased (see Table 4; see also Table 5 and Figure 1 on the repartition of pupils and students in the Danish education system).

Figure 1. **The present and the future subjects of the *Folkeskole* and their distribution on form 1 to 10**

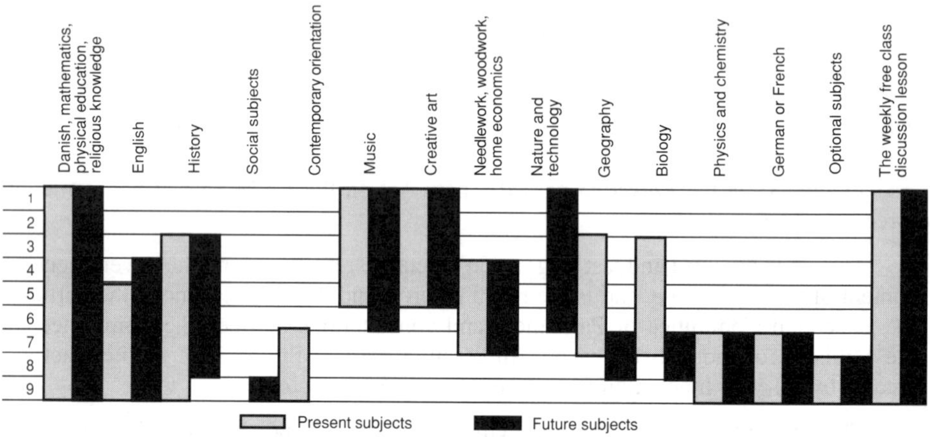

Source: Danish Ministry of Education (1994), *Danish Youth Education, Problems and Achievements.*

Table 4. **Number of weekly lessons in the *Folkeskole***

	The present minimum	The future minimum
1-2 Forms	15	20
3 Form	18	22
4 Form	20	24
5 Form	23	24
6-7 Forms	23	26
8-9-10 Forms	24	28

Source: Danish Ministry of Education (1994), *Danish Youth Education, Problems and Achievements.*

The *Gymnasium* in its Present Form

According to the present Act from 1990 the *Gymnasium* offers three years of upper secondary education in two streams: the linguistic and the mathematical streams.

A more detailed description of the present *Gymnasium* system is given in Chapter 4. "Upper secondary education" also contains a description of the Higher Preparatory Examination course (HF) and the Higher commercial and Higher technical examination courses (HHX and HTX) are offered by the commercial and technical schools mentioned below.

Vocational Education and Training

A detailed description of the present system according to the 1989 Act on Vocational Education, which came into force on 1 January 1991, is given in Chapter 4 (see "Vocationally oriented education"). This chapter also describes other vocational oriented types of youth education.

Post-secondary and Higher Education

Danish higher education — or post-secondary education — is divided into three categories: short higher education (one to two years, non-university level), medium long higher education (three to four years, non-university, as well as university level) and long higher education (five years and more, university level).

Study programmes

In most cases, the study programmes at university level resemble the study programmes of most other European countries. The periods of study are generally rather long. Most programmes leading to a Master's degree take five or six years. It has, however, recently become possible to complete a 3-year study programme with a Bachelor's degree at Danish universities.

Institutions of higher education

The following twelve institutions of higher education at university level exist: the universities of Copenhagen, Aarhus, Odense, Aalborg and Roskilde, Denmark's Technical University, the Royal Veterinary and Agricultural University, the Royal Danish School of Pharmacy, the business schools of Copenhagen, Aarhus and South-Jutland and the Royal Danish School of Educational Studies.

More than 100 institutions offer short or medium long higher education at non-university level: 60 colleges of education, the Engineering Academy, eight colleges of engineering (teknika), the Graphic College, three schools of social work, eleven colleges of socio-educational training, the School of Advanced Training of Social

Pedagogues and a number of schools for different categories of health personnel. Finally the technical and commercial schools offer short higher education courses of 1$^1/_2$-2 years duration (*cf.* Chapter 4).

The Ministry of Cultural Affairs runs the following institutions of higher education: the Royal Academy of Fine Arts, two schools of architecture, five academies of music and the Royal School of Librarianship.

Adult Education and Training

Danish adult education has its roots in the concept of *folkeoplysning* — popular enlightenment —which again has its origin in the 19th century's religious and social movements. During the first decades of the 20th century adult education was based upon general leisure-time education as it was offered by the adult education associations through their evening courses.

The serious unemployment situation in the thirties and forties created, however, an incipient understanding of the unskilled workers' need for improved qualifications.

In 1940 the unskilled workers' unions, the employers associations and the technological institutes established 3-year evening courses in the winter season for unskilled workers. In 1950 the Ministry of Labour stepped in and established five schools for unemployed, unskilled workers offering 3-week vocational day courses. The present legislation, the Act on Labour market Education and Training from 1985, comprises both courses for unskilled workers, supplementary training for skilled workers, technicians and supervisors and retraining for redeployment.

In addition to the Act on Labour Market Education and Training administrated by the Ministry of Labour, the Ministry of Education administrates the Act on Open Education from 1990, revised in 1993.

Qualifying general education for adults according to the Act on Formal Adult Education from 1989 is offered at approximately 80 adult education centres (VUC) run by the counties. At the centres, adults can follow single subject-courses leading to the leaving and advanced leaving examinations of the *Folkeskole* (LE and ALE) and to the Higher Preparatory Examination (HF).

The Danish Marking System

Where assessment of pupils and students is expressed with marks, the following marking scale shall be used: 13-11-10-9-8-7-6-5-3-0.

Concerning the use of the individual marks the following shall apply:

Group   Mark

Excellent
13: is given for the exceptionally independent and excellent performance;
11: is given for the independent and excellent performance;
10: is given for the excellent but not particularly independent performance.

Average
9: is given for the good performance, a little above average;
8: is given for the average performance;
7: is given for the mediocre performance, slightly below average.

Pass
6: is given for the somewhat hesitant but more or less satisfactory performance;

Hesitant
5: is given for the hesitant and not satisfactory performance;
3: is given for the very hesitant, very insufficient and unsatisfactory performance.

0: is given for the completely unacceptable performance.

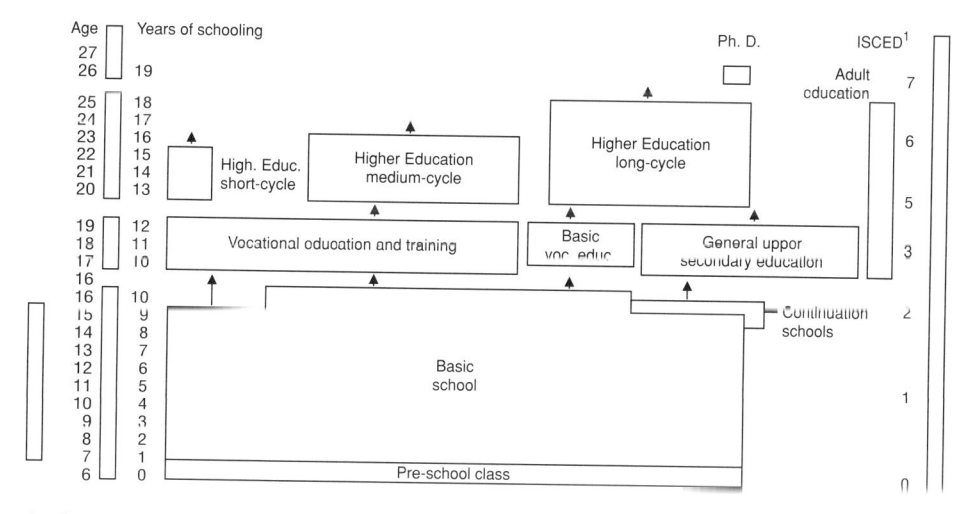

Figure 2. **The Danish education system**

1. International Standard Classification of Education.
Source: Danish Ministry of Education (1994), *Danish Youth Education, Problems and Achievements.*

Table 5. Pupils and students in the Danish educational system by age, sex and level of education, 1991

TOTAL M + F	Compulsory education	Upper sec. educ./gen.	Diploma courses II	Upper sec. educ./voc., 1st stage	Upper sec. educ./voc., 2nd stage	Higher educ. short-cycle	Higher educ. university, first degree	Higher educ. univ., final degree	Total
5-9	156 685	0	0	0	0	0	0	0	156 685
per cent	27.9	0.0	0.0	0.0	0.0	0.0	0.0	0.0	16.6
10-14	291 707	5	0	1	0	0	0	0	291 713
per cent	52.0	0.0	0.0	0.0	0.0	0.0	0.0	0.0	31.0
15-19	113 050	69 358	18 926	38 951	34 899	539	1 841	1 803	279 347
per cent	20.1	93.5	76.8	78.9	48.2	3.6	2.4	2.6	29.7
20-24	45	3 963	4 634	5 103	30 778	7 945	37 870	25 635	115 973
per cent	0.0	5.3	18.8	10.3	42.5	53.2	49.8	37.4	12.3
25-29	3	600	662	2 287	4 042	3 863	22 581	21 338	55 376
per cent	0.0	0.8	2.7	4.6	5.6	25.9	29.7	31.1	5.9
30 and above	9	273	427	3 043	2 633	2 576	13 684	19 801	42 456
per cent	0.0	0.4	1.7	6.2	3.6	17.3	18.0	28.9	4.5
Total	561 489	74 199	24 649	49 385	72 352	14 923	75 976	68 577	941 550
per cent	100.0	100.0	100.0	100.0	100.0	100.0	100.0	100.0	100.0

Table 5. **Pupils and students in the Danish educational system by age, sex and level of education, 1991** *(cont.)*

MALES	Compulsory education	Upper sec. educ./gen.	Diploma courses II	Upper sec. educ./voc., 1st stage	Upper sec. educ./voc., 2nd stage	Higher educ. short-cycle	Higher educ. university, first degree	Higher educ. univ., final degree	Total
5-9	78 343	0	0	0	0	0	0	0	78 343
per cent	27.7	0.0	0.0	0.0	0.0	0.0	0.0	0.0	16.6
10-14	145 342	1	0	1	0	0	0	0	145 344
per cent	51.4	0.0	0.0	0.0	0.0	0.0	0.0	0.0	30.8
15-19	58 882	27 503	9 145	20 177	25 000	224	902	1 042	142 875
per cent	20.8	92.4	75.2	87.4	54.2	2.9	2.8	2.8	30.3
20-24	23	1 814	2 386	1 804	18 012	4 038	15 521	14 162	57 760
per cent	0.0	6.1	19.6	7.8	39.0	52.1	47.5	37.6	12.2
25-29	2	303	404	585	1 989	2 141	10 438	11 942	27 804
per cent	0.0	1.0	3.3	2.5	4.3	27.6	31.9	31.7	5.9
30 and above	6	131	227	517	1 133	1 349	5 826	10 563	19 752
per cent	0.0	0.4	1.9	2.2	2.5	17.4	17.8	28.0	4.2
Total	282 598	29 752	12 162	23 084	46 134	7 752	32 687	37 709	471 878
per cent	100.0	100.0	100.0	100.0	100.0	100.0	100.0	100.0	100.0

Table 5. **Pupils and students in the Danish educational system by age, sex and level of education, 1991** *(cont.)*

FEMALES	Compulsory education	Upper sec. educ./gen.	Diploma courses II	Upper sec. educ./voc., 1st stage	Upper sec. educ./voc., 2nd stage	Higher educ. short-cycle	Higher educ. university, first degree	Higher educ. univ., final degree	Total
5-9	78 342	0	0	0	0	0	0	0	78 342
per cent	28.1	0.0	0.0	0.0	0.0	0.0	0.0	0.0	16.7
10-14	146 366	4	0	1	0	0	0	0	146 370
per cent	52.5	0.0	0.0	0.0	0.0	0.0	0.0	0.0	31.2
15-19	54 148	41 855	9 781	18 774	9 899	315	939	761	136 472
per cent	19.4	94.2	78.3	71.4	37.8	4.4	2.2	2.5	29.1
20-24	22	2 149	2 248	3 299	12 766	3 907	22 349	11 473	58 213
per cent	0.0	4.8	18.0	12.5	48.7	54.5	51.6	37.2	12.4
25-29	1	297	258	1 702	2 053	1 722	12 143	9 396	27 572
per cent	0.0	0.7	2.1	6.5	7.8	24.0	28.1	30.4	5.9
30 and above	13	142	200	2 526	1 500	1 227	7 858	9 238	22 704
per cent	0.0	0.3	1.6	9.6	5.7	17.1	18.2	29.9	4.8
Total	**278 392**	**44 447**	**12 487**	**26 301**	**26 218**	**7 171**	**43 289**	**30 868**	**469 673**
per cent	**100.0**	**100.0**	**100.0**	**100.0**	**100.0**	**100.0**	**100.0**	**100.0**	**100.0**

Source: Danish Ministry of Education (1994), *Danish Youth Education, Problems and Achievements.*

Chapter 3

THE DEVELOPMENT DURING THE LAST DECADE

During the last decade development and reforms of the Danish educational system have been carried through in accordance with the following guidelines:
- steering by targets and frameworks instead of detailed regulations;
- increased market orientation with user-influence through institutions boards and free choice of schools;
- switch-over to educational programmes with better employment prospects;
- focus on quality and internationalisation;
- educational programmes as open networks for young and adults;
- more efficiency and places for more students for less money.

Education and the Labour Market

Recent years have seen a significant reorganisation of both higher education and vocational education and training with the purpose of ensuring conformity between the qualifications of the graduates and the needs of the labour market.

The alternance principle of the vocational education and training courses provides a close connection to the labour market which is of great importance both to the relevance of the courses and to young people's choice of education and training and their adaptation to working life.

The same connection does normally not exist in higher education. This has *inter alia* meant that a system of regulation of admission has been necessary for a number of years — regulating not only the total intake but also part of the intake to the individual areas.

In the 1990s, the need for regulation of admission is less pronounced as a result of the structural reforms which are now in the process of being implemented in most educational areas. The courses have in general been given a broader scope and have been made more flexible enabling the students to leave earlier with a qualification — as it is the case with the Bachelor reform. At the same time, the Open Education system has improved the possibilities of returning at a later stage in order to supplement previous qualifications in a new form of alternance education.

The influx to the short-, medium- and long-cycle higher education courses aiming at the private business sector has almost doubled since the introduction of the general regulation of admission.

The regulations of admission to higher education have now been changed and emphasis is to a greater extent put on the real qualifications of the applicants. There will thus be a particular quota for which the criteria will be laid down by the individual institution and where emphasis will be put on what is actually required for completing a given course of study.

The number of applicants for the study places in higher education have, during the 1980s, grown from 26 200 in 1982 to 60 000 in 1991 (part of the increase can be explained by the fact that the definitions of study programmes belonging to the higher education sector have been substantially expanded). The capacity of higher education programmes — and how an expanded capacity can be obtained — have been recurrent political issues in the last half of the 1980s. The Parliament has granted funds for an expansion by 4 000 study places in 1991 and — after new negotiations between the government and opposition parties — a further 5 000 places in 1992. According to further agreements between the Government and the Parliament in 1992, provisions have been made for admission of 41 000 students per year in the period 1993-96.

New Mechanisms of Funding — The "Taximeter" System

The "taximeter" system is part of the Ministry's overall strategy: management by targets and framework. The "taximeter" system is based upon the allocation of grants to the institutions according to their level of activity: many students release a large grant, few students only release a small grant. A key element of the "taximeter" system is the block grant principle. As long as the block grant is used for legitimate purposes, the institution is free to spend the money in accordance with its own priorities.

In April 1989 the *Folketing* passed the present Act on Vocational Schools. This act *inter alia* introduced the "taximeter" system. According to the act each school receives an annual grant computed on objective criteria, *i.e.* the number of full-time students equivalents and rates fixed for the different trade courses offered by the school. The rates are approved by the Parliament and included in the appropriation act (*cf.* Chapter 4).

Since the beginning of the 1980s, allocation of funds to the universities and other institutions of higher education has been calculated by a computerised budget model. This model could be characterised as a semi-"taximeter" system.

Teaching grants were calculated on the basis of a forecast of the so-called study step increments (SSI), *i.e.* the number of passed examinations corresponding to the the study activity of one year. Based on the forecasted SSI the number of teachers, the number of support staff, the budget for equipment and teaching aids, etc., were decided. Standard rates for teachers salary and salary for the support staff were included in the model.

These calculations were made on faculty level. The forecast of SSI was based on the yearly enrolment, the historically known drop-out rates, and the average study time.

In addition to the teaching grants calculated in this way, the institutions received funds for research and joint purposes. These funds were fixed by the traditional incremental method.

From 1994 the appropriation is fixed according to pure "taximeter" principles similar to the system of the vocational schools.

In the spring of 1991, the *Folketing* passed a new private school act. It introduced a new public grant system for private schools giving them a grant for operational expenditures per pupil per year which in principle matches the public expenditures per pupil in the municipal schools — less the private school fees paid by the parents.

In 1993 a bill was passed based on the "taximeter" principles concerning grants to the Folk High Schools, Continuation Schools, Domestic Science Schools and Needlework Schools. The schools will receive a basic grant (independent of the number of pupils) and a rate per pupil dependent on teachers seniority.

Summary

From the fiscal year of 1994 all schools financed by the central government receive their grants based on various "taximeter" systems adapted to different types of schools including basic grants catering for small schools' viability.

Local government schools, *i.e.* municipal schools and county schools, are not financed according to "taximeter" systems. Local governments decide themselves on the system to use when financing these kinds of institutions, but the Ministry of Education has laid down certain minimum requirements.

The State Education Grant and Loan Scheme

In Denmark, a State educational support system has been in force since the 1950s. The support consists of a combination of grants and State loans. In 1988, the present education grant and loan scheme (including the voucher system) was introduced.

At the beginning of a study course (within the voucher system) the student receives a certain number of monthly "vouchers" corresponding to the officially stipulated time of the study programme. Each voucher gives the student the right to receive one month's grant (DKr 1 890 when the student lives with her/his parents, DKr 3 310 when the student lives away from home) and one month's State loan (DKr 1 489). If the student has received support (used vouchers) during a previous course, these used vouchers are deducted from the total number of vouchers for the new course.

The division into monthly grants and loans (vouchers) makes it possible for the students to take personal decisions as to when they want to use the vouchers. If the students know that they will have a bigger income from other sources than the so-called "free amount", they can save their vouchers for later. In the last period of their studies they may then use "double monthly vouchers". But if the student do not save the vouchers in a period when they make money in excess of the "free amount", the received grants must be repaid penny by penny.

Decentralisation of the Steering of the Programmes of Education

The most extensive reform of the control of the content and organisation of courses has been carried through in the area of vocational education and training. In this area, the Ministry's control confines itself to the laying down of general regulations regarding the courses — in co-operation with the Council for Vocational Education — and to the laying down of framework regulations for the individual courses according to decisions taken by the central trade committees. The very detailed curricula laid down at central level which existed previously have been liquidated.

Increased Decentralisation and Institutional Self-regulation

More flexible frames for teacher work loads

If the educational institutions are to have a real possibility of independently organising how teaching and other types of work are to be carried out at the individual institution, the extent of centrally fixed rules relating to the teachers' use of their working hours, including all types of reduction schemes, must be reduced drastically. The management of the individual institution shall have the freedom to organise and decide on the distribution of the teachers' tasks within the working hours. The staff shall of course — like in other undertakings — have the possibility of exerting a contributory influence on the organisation of the work.

Strengthened institutional management and school boards

When the competence to organise the courses and decide on their more detailed contents, and the competence to control the finances are decentralised to the individual schools and institutions, there will be a great need for strengthening the management of the schools and institutions in order to make local autonomy real.

The entire management system in the primary and lower secondary level — the *Folkeskole* — has been changed significantly in the direction of fewer decision-making levels. All schools have at the beginning of 1990 set up school boards with a majority of parent representatives one of whom is meant to chair the board.

At the overall level. the school board is to lay down the principles of the activities of the school within the targets and framework set out by the municipal council. The school board is *inter alia* to lay down the principles of the organisation of teaching, the number of lessons of the pupils, special education, the co-operation between the school and the parents, the orientation of the parents about the pupils' progress at school, the distribution of the work between the teachers as well as of joint arrangements for the pupils during school hours. The school board is also to approve the teaching materials, lay down the rules of conduct and approve the school's budget. Finally, the school board also makes proposals to the municipal council concerning the curricula of the school, non-course divided instruction and the appointment of head teachers and teachers. At the same time, the role of the individual head teacher has been strengthened significantly.

The reform of vocational education and training entails the most far-reaching strengthening of local management. It is first and foremost the board of the school which, in co-operation with the principal of the school and the local training committees, is to assume the many new tasks which have been decentralised from central level.

In connection with the negotiations regarding the new Act on the *Gymnasium* (general upper secondary school) the Association of County Councils and the Ministry of Education only agreed to recommend to the county councils that they allocate the grants to the individual school in the form of a block grant according to "taximeter" grant-awarding principles.

The new Act of 23 December 1992 on Universities is based on the following principles:

- massive authority transfer from the Ministry to the institutions;
- preservation of the institutional democracy, but a reduction of the number of governing bodies and their number of members in order to achieve a higher degree of decision-making ability;
- the rector will be responsible for the collective activities of the institution both internally and externally;
- the establishment of strengthened, unambiguous, and visible management authorities through delegation by the rector;
- separation of education management and research management;
- external representation in the main governing bodies (the senate and the faculty council).

The Project on Content and Quality Development

The cuts made in the public budgets and the necessary more intensive use of the educational resources in the 1980s brought the question of quality in education into focus. It became a matter of concern that the economic cut-back might lead to a reduction of the quality. In order to avoid this the Minister of Education in 1988 launched the project on content and quality development, which covered the entire educational system.

It was decided that the education system and its qualities should be evaluated from three angles:

- *horizontally*:   analysing each level of the system one by one;
- *vertically*:   assessing the subjects as they are taught at primary, secondary and tertiary levels with emphasis on the coherence, progression and the transition from one level to another;
- *institutionally*:   evaluation of individual institutions.

Committees consisting of specialists from all levels of the education system together with experts outside the school world have been and are set up for each subject making a report intended to serve as a basis for possible changes and improvements.

The committees describe and evaluate the subjects as they are taught at all levels of the Danish school system taking into consideration:

- how they are taught;
- how the pupils and students experience the progression;
- the teachers' qualifications;
- what weaknesses and problems have been detected;
- what suggestions for improvements can be made.

In Chapter 4 ("Upper secondary education"), a more thorough description of the quality development project in general upper secondary education is given.

The Centre for evaluation of higher education and the external examiners

Based upon the experience from *ad hoc* evaluations, it was decided in 1992 to establish a Centre for Evaluation of Higher Education. The centre is commissioned to initiate regular evaluations of the study programmes by teams of national and foreign experts in order to strengthen the quality of higher education at a high professional level. Furthermore it is the task of the centre to collect national and international experience in the field of evaluation of education and quality development and to ensure a dialogue between the centre, the institutions of higher education and the employers of the graduates.

The presidency of the five advisory boards of education in humanities, social sciences, medicine, natural sciences and technology forms the governing board of the centre.

In Denmark, external examiners are widely used at tests and exams, and the impartial and external professional evaluation of the level of the different programmes, which takes place on a regular basis anyway, will be incorporated in the central quality assessment.

The Costs of Education

In 1991, the total public expenditure on education amounted to approximately 58 billion DKr which were more or less equally distributed between the State on the one hand and the counties and municipalities on the other (see Tables 6 and 7).

Table 6. **Public expenditure for education and training by level of education, 1982-91**

1991 prices

	1982	1983	1984	1985	1986	1987	1988	1989	1990	1991
				Billion DKr						
Total	55.0	55.4	55.3	55.5	56.4	53.0	58.8	59.7	58.4	57.7
Basic school education	27.9	27.0	27.0	27.3	27.2	28.0	27.6	27.2	26.2	25.7
Youth education	11.2	11.5	11.5	11.1	11.3	12.1	12.4	13.0	12.9	13.0
Higher education*	9.6	9.9	9.9	10.1	10.6	10.0	10.6	11.0	10.9	10.6
Adult education	4.6	5.0	5.0	5.3	5.5	6.1	6.2	6.8	6.6	6.8
Administration, help services, etc.	1.7	1.9	1.9	1.8	1.8	1.9	2.0	1.8	1.7	1.6

* The State Educational Support System included. Research expenses excluded.
Source: Danish Ministry of Education (1994), *Danish Youth Education, Problems and Achievements*.

Table 7. **Expenditure on the State Educational Support System, 1981/82 - 1990/91**
1991 prices

	81/82	82/83	83/84	84/85	85/86	86/87	87/88	88/89	89/90	90/91
					Billion DKr					
Total expenditure										
Grants	2.1	2.2	2.3	2.4	2.4	2.4	2.8	4.5	4.4	4.4
State-guaranteed loans	1.4	0.9	0.8	0.8	0.8	0.8	0.6	0.1	0.1	0.1
State loans	—	0.5	0.6	0.6	0.6	0.6	0.7	1.3	1.2	1.1
Total	3.5	3.6	3.8	3.8	3.8	3.8	4.1	5.9	5.6	5.6
Of which:										
Youth education	1.1	1.2	1.2	1.3	1.2	1.2	1.2	1.9	1.7	1.5
Higher education	2.4	2.5	2.6	2.6	2.6	2.6	2.9	4.0	3.9	4.1
Expenditure per support recipient										
					1 000 DKr					
Youth education										
Grants	14.9	14.0	14.0	14.4	15.0	15.3	15.8	20.6	19.9	18.7
State-guaranteed loans	19.9	15.5	16.1	16.0	16.5	15.8	14.5	—	—	—
State loans	—	8.9	8.9	9.0	9.3	9.3	9.7	14.5	14.2	12.4
Higher education										
Grants	20.6	21.2	21.5	21.7	21.8	21.7	23.0	33.9	32.4	30.9
State-guaranteed loans	25.7	19.3	19.8	19.8	20.0	19.0	19.0	46.1	37.7	33.5
State loans/study loans	—	10.8	10.9	11.0	11.0	11.0	11.5	17.5	16.1	14.7

Source: Danish Ministry of Education (1994), *Danish Youth Education, Problems and Achievements*.

The 58 billion DKr for education and research correspond to approximately 6.8 per cent of the GDP (see Tables 8 and 9).

Table 8. **Expenditure on education and training in per cent of the GDP, public expenditure on education and training in per cent of the total public expenditure, and the total public expenditure in per cent of the GDP in Denmark and other OECD countries, 1991**

	Exp. on education			Publ. exp. for educ. in relation to total publ. exp.	Total public exp. in relation to GDP
	Public	Private	Total		
	(% of GDP)			%	
OECD average	5.2	1.4	6.4	12.8	40.0
Denmark	6.1	0.0	6.1	10.4	58.7
Norway	6.8	—	—	12.1	55.5
Sweden	6.5	0.5	6.5	10.4	61.5
Finland	6.1	0.5	6.6	14.7	47.2
Germany	4.0	1.5	5.4	8.0	48.7
United Kingdom	5.3	—	—	12.5	40.8
Ireland	5.5	0.4	5.9	—	42.9
Netherlands	5.6	0.1	5.8	9.8	54.4
Belgium	5.4	—	—	9.5	50.0
Luxemburg	—	—	—	—	—
France	5.4	0.6	6.0	10.6	50.6
Switzerland	5.4	—	—	15.9	—
Austria	5.4	—	—	10.8	49.8
Italy	—	—	—	—	53.6
Spain	4.5	1.1	5.6	—	43.3
Portugal	5.5	—	—	—	44.7
United States	5.5	1.5	7.0	14.7	34.2
Canada	6.7	0.7	7.4	13.8	48.8
Australia	4.7	0.8	5.5	12.6	36.7
Japan	3.7	1.3	5.0	11.4	31.4

Sources: *OECD Economic Outlook* (1993), No 53, June, OECD, Paris, p. 215
Education at a Glance — OECD Indicators (1993), OECD, Paris, 1993.
Danish Ministry of Education (1994), *Danish Youth Education, Problems and Achievements*.

Choices and Networks — New Concepts in Education

Free choice of education

The free choice of school and education is of central importance to a well-functioning education system. Apart from the fact that it is a goal in itself to give the students a free choice, a free choice of school and education will also further the schools' initiative and industry.

The free choice of school has therefore been introduced in the field of vocational education and training, and it has been cemented in the field of upper

Table 9. Pupil/teacher ratio and average number of pupils per class distributed on types of instructions, 1982/83 - 1991/92

	82/83	83/84	84/85	85/86	86/87	87/88	88/89	89/90	90/91	91/92
					Pupil/teacher ratio					
Basic school										
The *Folkeskole*	11.9	11.9	11.6	11.3	10.9	10.6	10.3	10.3	10.1	10.3
Private schools	12.7	12.6	12.5	12.3	11.9	11.6	11.6	11.6	11.8	11.2
Youth education										
The *Gymnasium*	10.2	10.2	10.4	10.3	10.1	10.0	9.8	9.8	9.5	9.2
Commercial schools	—	—	—	—	12.2	12.1	12.4	12.5	12.5	12.4
Technical schools	—	—	—	—	8.0	7.6	7.4	7.8	8.6	8.9
Higher education										
Weighted average	9.7	10.1	10.7	10.8	11.3	11.9	11.8	12.2	13.0	13.6
Humanities	11.3	12.8	12.2	12.5	13.0	13.2	13.0	13.8	14.8	16.5
Health sciences	—	—	—	9.6	9.8	9.9	9.4	9.5	9.9	10.4
Natural sciences	6.9	6.9	7.7	7.5	7.9	8.3	8.2	8.7	9.4	9.9
Social sciences	15.9	16.3	17.7	17.8	18.9	20.2	19.6	20.1	21.3	22.0
Technical courses	6.8	7.2	8.1	8.1	8.7	9.3	9.4	9.4	10.1	10.2
Teacher training	—	—	—	—	8.7	8.8	9.2	9.8	10.2	10.9
of which: Colleges of educ.	—	—	—	—	6.1	6.0	6.6	7.8	8.0	8.5
				Normal number of pupil per class						
Basic school										
The *Folkeskole*	18.2	18.2	18.1	18.0	18.0	17.9	18.1	18.2	18.2	18.4
Private schools	16.2	16.0	16.2	16.2	16.2	15.8	16.3	15.8	15.9	15.6
Youth education										
The *Gymnasium*	23.0	23.3	23.4	23.3	22.7	—	23.2	23.6	23.9	—

Source: Danish Ministry of Education (1994), *Danish Youth Education, Problems and Achievements*.

secondary education. In the field of primary and lower secondary education, where private independent schools have always constituted a real alternative — which now attract approximately 10 per cent of the pupils within the compulsory school age — recent legislative changes have given the municipalities the freedom to introduce a free choice of school from among the schools of the municipality.

Open education

With the introduction of Open Education in 1990, the Danish tradition of adults qualifying themselves in their leisure time has caught on with renewed strength. A new Act on Open Education was issued on 30 June 1993.

Open Education aims at enabling the entire adult population to qualify themselves concurrently with their own wishes and occupational needs and is based on the principle of life-long — or recurrent — education. In principle it makes the same courses and programmes available to adults as those offered to young people in the ordinary educational system. A subject passed under Open Education automatically gets full credit in the ordinary programme to which it belongs. This means that one can combine subjects passed under Open Education with subjects passed as a part of an ordinary programme. It is also possible to piece together subjects passed solely under Open Education to a total qualifying education.

Institutions offering Open Education courses receive a fixed grant per student full-time equivalent, and in addition to that they may charge a fee. The state subsidy normally corresponds approximately 80 per cent of the fair standard gross expenses of the education programme as presupposed by the State.

Internationalisation of Danish Education

In a small country with a very high level of foreign trade, with a geographical position as a European crossroad and a population of 5 million speaking its own national language the surrounding world and the teaching of foreign languages have to play an important role in the curricula of the component parts of the educational system. An EU survey[1] has shown that 95 per cent of Danish youth under 25 have conversational ability in English, while 67 per cent have the same ability in German.

In the *Folkeskole* international topics are dealt with in history, geography and contemporary orientation, but in subjects like Danish literature, biology, art and music an international aspect may also be adopted in order to put the teaching into a broader perspective and to widen the pupils' horizon. In the 7th-10th form more than 90 per cent of the pupils spend 25 per cent of their lessons learning English and German/French.

In Danish foreign language teaching the languages is not only regarded as a medium of communication. It also contributes to the creation of international understanding by providing knowledge about the culture, the way of life and the traditions of the country where the language is spoken.

In the *Gymnasium* — but to a lesser degree at the HF-courses — there has been a tradition for going on study tours abroad long before internationalisation of education was on the agenda. These study tours normally go to one of the countries whose language the pupils are learning, but other subjects like Danish, classical civilisation history, geography and physics also use study tours abroad as a part of the education.

In history and geography working with historical and geographical topics in other countries is an essential part, and in Danish a part of the literature read must be translated world literature.

At the coming into force of the Act on Vocational Education in 1991 the international aspect became much more important at the commercial schools and two foreign languages are now compulsory subjects.

The description of the other subjects is marked by international aspects to a higher degree than previously. In approximately 2/3 of the basic subjects the international element forms an important part of the subject descriptions.

At the revision of the Higher Commercial Examination course (HHX) in 1991 the international element was also strengthened. Two foreign languages are compulsory and during the second course year the students have to write a bigger paper based upon one of the subjects with an international element.

The new short higher education of market economists is international in its approach and intended to come up to the best European courses at the same level. Each student has *inter alia* to do a 5-week project study abroad.

The new Act on Vocational Education presupposes that the technical schools teach the internationally most relevant production and manufacturing methods and give the students a relatively broad basic knowledge and routine to be used also at further education abroad. Thus 2/3 of the trade-programmes include foreign languages as a compulsory subject and it is now possible for the students to spend some or all of their trainee periods at enterprises in the EU and EFTA countries, which gives vocational education a new international element.

As far as higher education is concerned internationalisation is not a new idea. Many studies have very old traditions for stays abroad as a normal integrated part of the study. Studies of foreign languages is of course one example, but a number of other studies, for example the classical studies, have since long had an international dimension.

Internationalisation did not, however, get a central role in education policy until the big mobility programmes like ERASMUS, COMETT and LINGUA were launched by EU in the 1980s. In order to avoid an EU-monopolisation of international education activities the government in the mid-80s decided to grant considerable means for international activities with countries outside the EU, primarily the United States, Canada, Japan and the EFTA countries.

Finally the Nordic Council of Ministers in 1988 adopted the NORDPLUS programme — an internordic exchange — and a study programme for students and teachers at upper secondary and tertiary levels. An action plan on co-operation (including expansion of the NORDPLUS programme and a convention on admission to higher education) has been adopted in 1991 by the Nordic countries and another one is on the planning stage in the European Union based *inter alia* on the Commission's Memorandum on Higher Education.

Reference

1. "Young Europeans", report undertaken on behalf of Task Force for "Human Resources, Education, Training and Youth" by INRA (Europe), European Co-ordination Office SA/NV, May 1991.

Chapter 4

YOUTH EDUCATION

As it can be seen from Table 10, 93 per cent of the young people who have finished their compulsory education continue in the youth education system. Of these 93 per cent, 33 per cent are admitted at general upper secondary education, while nearly 60 per cent begin a vocational education programme.

Vocationally Oriented Education

Historical development of vocational education schemes

The period up to 1870

Apprenticeship training in a well organised form has its origin in the medieval guilds. Economic and political liberalism in the first half of the 19th century led, however, to a demand for the abolition of the guild system, and the guilds were deprived of their rights by the 1857 Act on the Freedom of Trade. The freedom of trade was a real threat to the craft occupations, and associations were formed to defend the crafts all over the country. For these associations, the establishment and operation of technical schools was a natural focus. Thus, as early as in 1870, about 50 technical schools were established by local craft and industrial associations.

The period 1870-1960

From 1875, the government and subsequently the municipalities provided substantial grants for the setting up of technical and commercial schools with the result that in 1910 the number of technical schools was about 170. With the 1889 Apprenticeship Act (*Lærlingelov*), the situation of the apprentices was regulated again — the contractual relationship between master craftsmen and apprentices was *inter alia* reintroduced.

Industrialisation resulted in radical changes in the labour market. In the 1880s, local trade unions were formed, combined in national trade federations, which from 1898 were amalgamated in the Danish Federation of Trade Unions. The employers' side

Table 10. **Proportion of young people who continue in general upper secondary education or vocational education after basic school distributed, by sex, 1981/82 - 1990/91**

	81/82	82/83	83/84	84/85	85/86	86/87	87/88	88/89	89/90	90/91
					%					
All	89	88	88	90	91	92	92	92	93	93
General upper secondary education	32	32	31	31	32	32	32	33	33	34
Vocational education	54	55	56	58	59	59	59	59	59	59
Others	1	1	1	1	0	0	1	0	0	0
Men	88	89	88	90	91	91	91	91	92	92
General upper secondary education	26	25	24	25	25	25	25	25	26	26
Vocational education	61	63	64	65	66	65	66	66	66	66
Others	0	2	0	0	0	0	0	0	0	0
Women	87	87	89	90	91	92	93	93	93	94
General upper secondary education	39	40	39	38	39	39	40	41	41	43
Vocational education	46	47	49	50	51	52	52	52	51	51
Others	1	1	1	1	1	1	1	1	1	0

Source: Danish Ministry of Education (1994), *Danish Youth Education, Problems and Achievements.*

formed similar employers' associations during this period, which in 1898 merged into the Danish Employers' and Master Craftsmen's Association. This institutional framework became very important for the further development of vocational training. In the 1920s, the first trade committee was formed, in which the organisations of the master craftsmen, on a par with the trade unions, dealt with questions relating to apprenticeship training schemes, including school matters.

The 1956 Apprenticeship Act abolished the restriction on the number of apprentices — which must of course also be considered against the background of the industrial sector's urgent need for skilled labour. Dissatisfaction with the teaching at technical schools was also increasing in the period prior to 1956. The instruction was now changed from evening classes to day classes with completely new course requirements.

The period 1960-1987

The 1960s were a period of strong economic growth. For the manufacturing industry in particular — which needed all-round, mobile and more specialised labour — the Act of 1956 was out-of-date. More and more young people chose an academic education, and the number of students entering apprenticeship training schemes was insufficient to meet the demand for skilled labour. In order to meet this demand, attempts were made in the early 1970s to set up a new structure for initial training schemes.

In 1977 the Basic Vocational Education Act (the EFG-Act) was passed. The crucial new element in EFG, compared with the apprenticeship training scheme, was that the courses started with a whole year at a technical or commercial school. Within this period, a broad introduction was given to a whole "family" of vocational training courses.

It was assumed that the apprenticeship training courses based on the apprenticeship-with-an-employer-principle would stop completely no later than 1982; but this did not happen. The decision to abandon the apprenticeship programmes was to be made by the individual trade committee, and only a few did this. As a consequence, there were two parallel systems of vocational training in Denmark in the 1980s and between the two systems, both the training structure and the management and counselling structure differed.

The 1989 reform

In May 1986, the Minister of Education therefore appointed a committee to propose a revision of the basic vocational training schemes, and a new Act on Vocational Education and Training based on the recommendations of the committee, was passed in Parliament by a very broad majority on 30 March 1989 — exactly one hundred years after the adoption of the first apprenticeship act in Denmark. An Act on Vocational Schools was passed on the same day. According to this, all vocational schools were fully privatised as non-profit organisations. The new acts have been in force since January 1991.

The Act on Vocational Education and Training replaced the 1956 Apprenticeship Act and the EFG-Act and constitutes the overall framework for the technical and vocational education sector, which has so far been covered by the apprenticeship training courses, the basic vocational education and training courses (EFG) and the basic technical education courses (*e.g.* laboratory technicians and technical assistants). A common set of rules now exists for these training courses.

One combined system has thus been established for all basic vocational education and training courses at the commercial and technical schools. These courses, of which there are now about 87, including a number of new streams (as against close to 300 in the past), are organised as alternance ("sandwich" training) courses, where periods of school-based education alternate with periods of practical training in a firm. The restriction of admission has (almost) been abandoned, and students and employers have been offered a free choice of school. All training courses lead to a skilled worker's certificate.

As it will appear, a great variety still prevails in the educational provision, which reflects the policy of the system to reach the widest range of youth groups possible. At the same time a diversified education and training system makes for greater flexibility in the adjustments that have to be undertaken on a current basis.

The trade committees perform a central role in relation to the curricula. They are responsible for modernising the training part of the courses with regard to the professional contents and for setting the standards of apprentices' final examinations. They also influence the academic side of the training by choosing the general subjects for which the Ministry has the responsibility of setting standards. With regard to the practical in-company training they set up rules for the training.

General education and vocational training

According to the Act on Vocational Education and Training, the education system should:

1) motivate young persons for education and ensure that all young people, who want to get a vocational qualification, have genuine possibilities of choosing between several different streams;

2) provide young people with a basis for future employment and at the same time contribute to personal development and understanding of society and its development;

3) meet the needs of the labour market for vocational and general qualifications assessed with a view to the development of business, production and society, including the development in the structure of the business sector, in labour market conditions, in workplace organisation and in technology; and

4) provide the youth with a solid basis for further education and training.

Access routes and training structure

Admission to a vocational training course is open to persons who have completed compulsory education and is not granted on the basis of certificates.

There are two routes into vocational training, *i.e.* the "school route" and the "practical training route". The two access routes meet at the commencement of the 2nd school period. Irrespective of the choice of access route, the duration and content of the training are the same.

Students choosing the "school route" normally enter the 1st school period, which lasts 20 weeks. Here, the students try out several different trade areas and receive parallel individual and collective vocational and educational guidance. Workshop training has a central role and is supplemented by more theoretical subjects. One third of the teaching hours consists of optional subjects. After the 1st school period, the students choose their specific stream and continue with the 2nd school period (also 20 weeks). After the 2nd school period, the students must enter into a training agreement with a firm for the practical training to continue their programme. The students receive a salary from the day they commence the practical training. Students who choose the "practical training route" receive a salary throughout their education and their first school-based training is the 2nd school period.

The admission figures for 1991 show that about 75 per cent of the students admitted to the technical schools have chosen the "school route" (Table 11).

In just under one third of the vocational trades, however, the 1st school period is optional. In these cases, the students may start directly on the 2nd school period. Students over 18 years of age may start directly on the 2nd school period. Adults with a relevant employment and training background are given credit for their qualifications (Figure 3).

The basic structure of the training schemes is based on the alternance ("sandwich"-course) training principle. The programmes are generally no longer than 4 years. Normally, the duration of the school period cannot exceed 80 weeks, including the 1st school period. The more detailed structure — alternation between school and practical training — is laid down by the trade committees. The duration of the total school attendance as part of a programme is, however, decided by the Ministry of Education.

The contract between employer and trainee

The training agreement is a contract which binds the student and the business enterprise(s) responsible for the practical training of the student. The agreement covers all practical training and school periods of the programme, including the journeyman's test, if any. The training agreement will always be a written agreement drawn up on a form which has been approved by the Minister. If the student is a minor, the parents must give their consent to the training agreement.

Table 11. **Intake to vocational education and training**

	1982	1984	1986	1988	1990	1991
Vocational education and training:						
Commerce and cleric. trades	24 569	24 271	24 351	26 825	24 257	22 581[1]
— School way	22 198	21 479	20 278	23 351	22 354	—
— Pract. training way	2 371	2 792	4 073	3 474	1 903	—
Technical trades	25 551	27 687	30 108	27 968	28 284	26 618[2]
— School way	14 859	16 595	16 373	17 151	19 326	—
— Pract. training way	10 692	11 092	13 735	10 817	8 958	—
Other programmes:						
Maritime education	938	929	731	631	436	442*
Agricultural education	2 200	2 300	1 700	1 200	1 850	1 745
Social and health education	3 288	3 742	3 877	3 718	2 929	6 100
Basic Techn., EDP-Ass.[3]	3 808	4 829	4 553	5 594	5 784	2 842
Other[4]	1 108	1 068	834	594	382	360*
Vocational education and training, total	61 462	64 826	66 154	66 530	63 922	60 688

Notes:
* Projected figures.
1. As the educational structure was characterised by transition schemes in 1991 after the implementation of the reform, the figure relating to the new intake is computed. The statistics for the first year of the 1980s are inadequate. The Department of Vocational Education and Training's estimate of the intake has therefore been used.
2. Has been partly included under vocational education and training from 1991.
3.
4. Comprises courses for ship's engineers, ship's cooks as well as civil service courses, etc.

Source: Danish Ministry of Education (1994), *Danish Youth Education, Problems and Achievements*.

Figure 3. **Vocational education and training**
Technical and business colleges

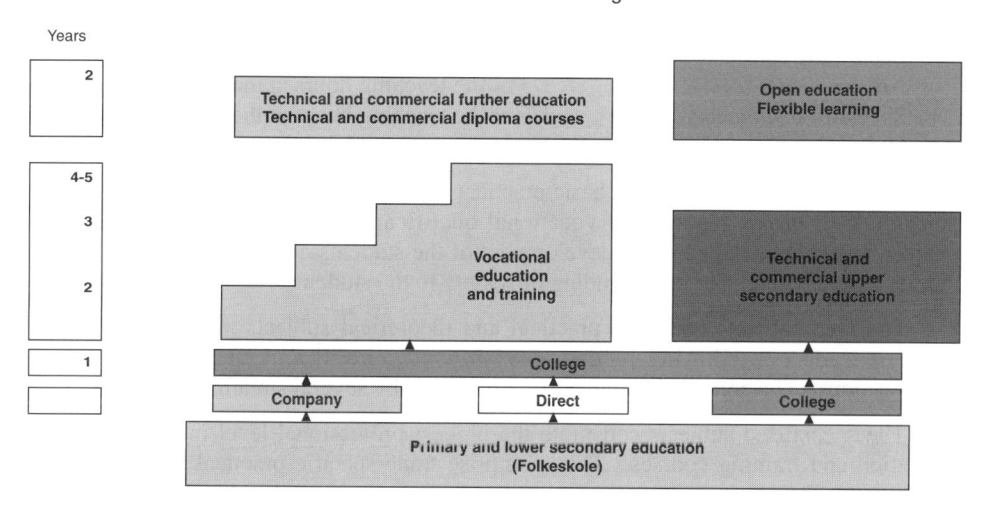

Source: Danish Ministry of Education (1994), *Danish Youth Education, Problems and Achievements..*

The practical training of a student may take place in several businesses. When this is the case, the school and practical training periods in which the individual business takes part must appear from the training agreement.

As a main rule, the student shall during his/her practical training be subject to the employment and working conditions which are laid down in the collective agreements or in the legislation in force. The training agreement contains information on the salary which the practical training business must pay the student during the practical training periods and the school periods which are comprised by the agreement.

The commercial and clerical sector

There are still two access routes into the system. The "school route" is organised as a combined 1st and 2nd school period comprising 40 weeks of schooling. The "practical training route" is based on a training agreement with a firm from the start. During the first year of practical training, the student frequently attends the school, for 18 weeks in total — often organised as two days at school and three days of practical in company training per week. After the first year, all students receive the same training, regardless of their access route (Figure 4).

The curricula

The curricula contain four different types of subjects:

Basic subjects:	1/3 of the teaching hours at the school
Area subjects:	1/3 of the teaching hours at the school
Specialised subjects:	1/6 of the teaching hours at the school
Optional subjects:	1/6 of the teaching hours at the school

The basic subjects comprise basic practical and theoretical instruction providing the students with broad general and vocational qualifications. It is the aim of the basic subjects to enhance the personal development of the students, to qualify them for further studies and to convey an understanding of society to the students.

The area subjects comprise practical and theoretical subjects relevant to a broad field of trade contributing to the provision of general and specific vocational qualifications. The area subjects are normally shared by several streams.

The specialised subjects constitute the highest professional level in the vocational education and training courses. They comprise trade-specific practical and theoretical instruction. The students choose a specialisation among the subjects which have been approved for the course in question. The choice of specialisation is normally included in the training agreement and relevant to the firm in question.

Figure 4. **Commercial education and training**
Business colleges

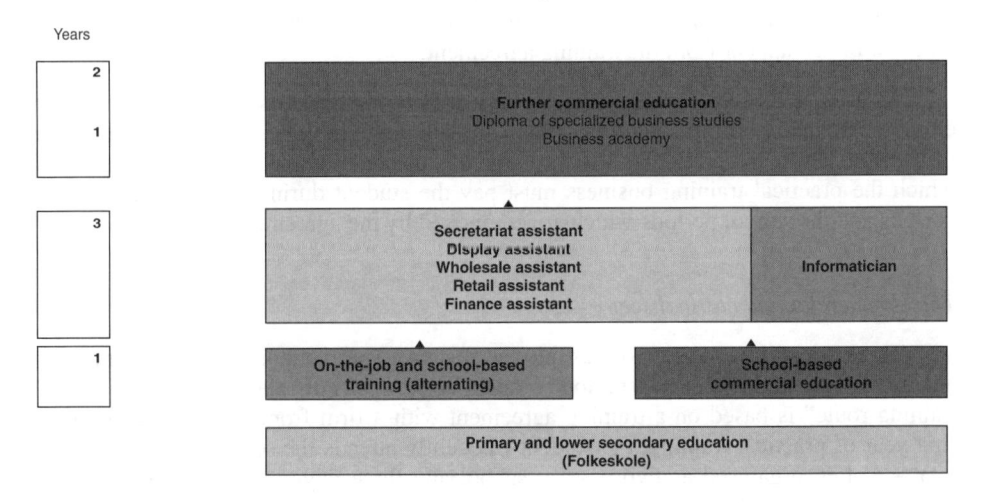

Source: Danish Ministry of Education (1994), *Danish Youth Education, Problems and Achievements.*

Syllabuses and examinations

The targets and general frames of the individual training courses are specified in administrative orders. These are drawn up by the Ministry of Education based on the input from the central trade committees. The administrative orders specify the basic subjects, area subjects and special subjects of the training course and include the targets which the students should attain in the various subjects as well as provisions as to how the assessment should be made.

Syllabuses containing the actual description of the content of the instruction are drawn up locally. The specific content of the instruction as well as the methods of instruction may vary from school to school.

The element of assessment has been strengthened in the courses. The performance of the students are subject to continuous assessment. The students complete their education by passing a final examination or trade test. The examination form varies from course to course, and it may have the form of a journeyman's test, a school examination or a combination of the two.

Technical vocational training schemes — examples

The individual education courses "stand alone"; but in fact they often share all the basic subjects and most of the area subjects. This ensures the flexibility and the broad perspective of the courses (Figure 5).

Vocational guidance

All activities concerning vocational guidance share a common legal basis, *i.e.* the Act on Educational and Vocational Guidance from 1981. Responsibility is shared between national, regional and local authorities, in close co-operation with the social partners, and is carried out in institutions under the Ministry of Labour and the Ministry of Education. The authorities and the social partners are represented in the National Council for Educational and Vocational Guidance (RUE), set up under this act, thus ensuring (among other things) that the needs of the labour market are taken into consideration as far as possible.

In general vocational guidance is considered a pedagogical task in Denmark. This means it is an important factor in every (vocational) school. In addition to the guidance of students in schools the recent reform of vocational education has stressed the importance of external guidance, which means that anybody interested can call or visit the school's guidance office. Guidance in schools is integrated in the curriculum. Part of the job is support of students trying to get a contractual training agreement. This purpose is a very important task for the school.

Figure 5. **The mechanical engineering course including specialisations**

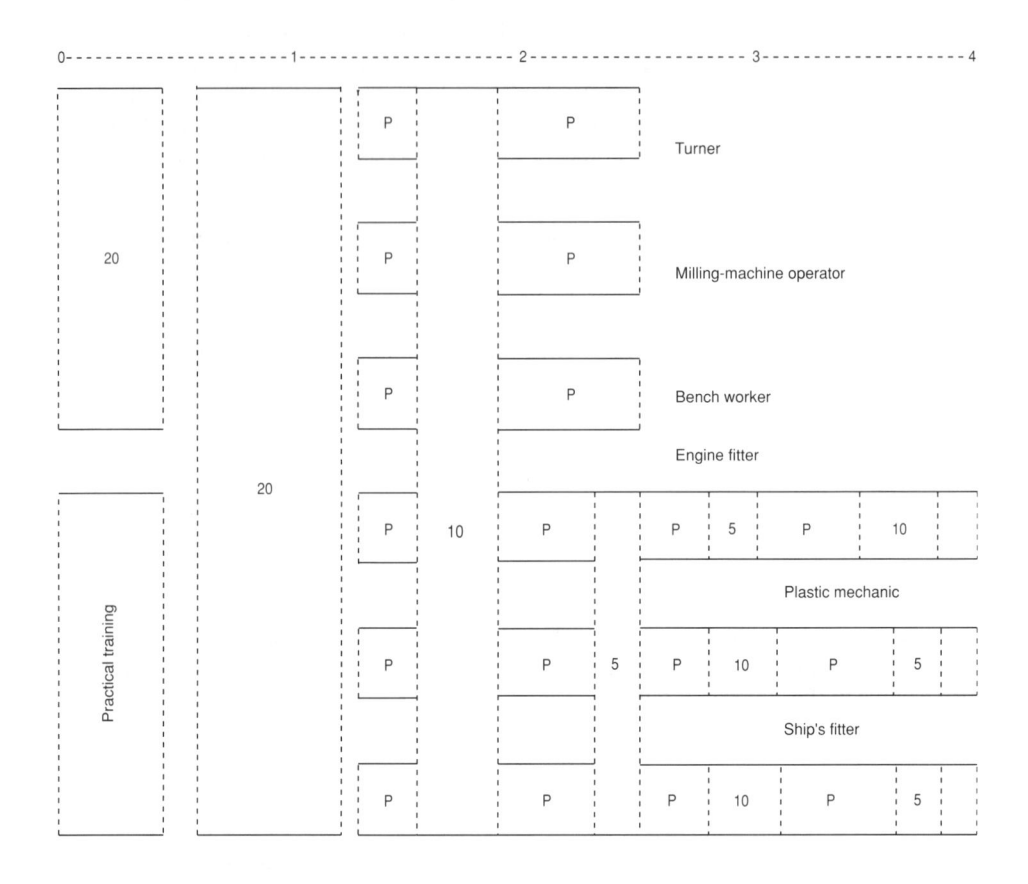

P: Practical training.

1) 1st school period (20 weeks) or 1st practical training period.
2) 2nd school period, 20 weeks.
3) 2nd practical training period, approx. 25 weeks.
4) 3rd school period, 10 weeks.
5) 3rd practical training period, approx. 25 weeks. For the specialisation of turner, milling-machine operator and bench worker until the end of the fixed course duration.
6) 4th school period, 5 weeks.
7) 4th practical training period, approx. 30 weeks.
8) 5th school period, 5 weeks, engine fitter.
9) 5th school period, 10 weeks, plastic mechanic and ship's fitter.
10) 5th practical training period, approx. 30 weeks.
11) 6th school period, 10 weeks, engine fitter.
12) 6th school period, 5 weeks, plastic mechanic and ship's fitter.
13) 6th practical training period, until the end of the fixed course duration.

Note: The programme is completed by an examination (journeyman's test) which is carried out in connection with the final school period.

Source: Danish Ministry of Education (1994), *Danish Youth Education, Problems and Achievements*.

Access to further education

Further technical education

The technicians' courses are offered at technical schools in continuation of the relevant vocational education and training courses. They are primarily aiming at employment comprising tasks relating to the following functions: construction, technical specification and technical descriptions, production planning, methodological development, product development, quality control, production and systems planning, etc. The courses are normally of 1^1/$_2$ years' duration.

The functions of a technician are relatively specialised compared to those of the chartered engineer. At the same time, however, it is presumed that the individual technician possesses a great ability to adapt, for instance in relation to technological changes. Technicians in many cases take part in product development, product control and administration as well as personnel management.

In order to be admitted to the further technical courses, graduates from the *Gymnasium* must complete a supplementary programme — either in the form of a 1-year workshop school or in the form of a 6-month workshop course both followed by one year of practical training in a firm. HTX graduates only have to complete the practical training period. The annual intake to the technicians' courses is approximately 4 000 students distributed on 25 different courses and specialisations.

Further commercial education

- The study programme in market economy

The aims of the subjects taught in this course are in particular reflecting the intended functions and tasks of the future graduates: sales and marketing functions in international markets, tasks of a co ordinating nature in and between the marketing, production and financial functions of the business as well as tasks as a qualified home base for staff stationed abroad. Another central aim of the course is that the students acquire a basis for further personal development with a view to enabling them to surmount linguistic and cultural barriers in connection with international marketing.

The 2-year programme is post-secondary and based on graduation from the *Gymnasium* or HHX. The third term of the second year is devoted to a study period abroad and to the student's subsequent work with the final main thesis. The programme is taught at the commercial schools.

- The study programmes at the commercial academies

There are at present approximately 25 commercial academies in Denmark, and they can be found within such different categories as tourism, international marketing, retailing, logistics, service and marketing as well as advertising and communication.

The duration of the commercial academy programmes may vary between one and three years. Typically, they are of 2 years' duration. The programmes are built on the concept of "sandwich" courses. Access is not limited to specific graduates of other education programmes, but practical training placement is a necessary condition for enrolment.

- The study programme for computer specialists

It is the aim of the subjects taught in the study programme for computer specialists that the students become able to work independently on the development, acquisition, and maintenance of computer systems with a special emphasis on the study programme's relevance to the business world.

The study programme comprises the following areas: the basics of computer science, the development of computer-based systems in businesses, specialised topics, and projects. The programme consists of five terms, totalling 27 months. The programme of the first three terms is compulsory, whereas the fourth term consists of a number of options. The fifth term is a project-term made in co-operation with the local business sector.

Graduates from the computer assistants programme and from the *Gymnasium*, HHX and HTX are admitted.

The Vocational School Act

Act no. 210 of 5 April 1989 on vocational schools established a new management system for the vocational schools and was the first consistent implementation of the target and framework control mentioned in Chapter 3.

The management of the school

The board is responsible for the overall management of the school and upon recommendation of the principal it lays down the annual programme of the activities of the school and approves its budget and accounts. Upon recommendation of the principal, the board decides on which approved vocational education and training courses and other approved courses the school shall offer in its programme. The Minister of Education approves the courses offered by the school.

The board appoints and dismisses the principal and upon the recommendation of the principal it approves the appointment and dismissal of the other staff of the school. The board is responsible vis-à-vis the Minister of Education for the running of the school and for the administration of the government grants.

The day-to-day management of the school is taken care of by a principal who ensures:

— that the courses are conducted in accordance with the legislation in force,
— that the educational conditions are sound,
— that the budget approved by the board is being respected, and
— that the activities of the school as such are in compliance with the decisions and guidelines of the board.

- Market conditions — More possibilities for local decisions

The vocational education and training reform introduced free access to the vocational education and training courses and the schools now have to admit all applicants or refer them to other schools which offer the same course. With a few exceptions it is now up to the individual schools themselves to decide which courses and how many study places they want to offer.

The reform implied a desire to increase the schools' freedom to organise the teaching with a view to attaining the educational targets within the given financial framework. In order to achieve this, all central regulations regarding class sizes for example were abolished, and the regulations regarding the number of lessons of the students were modified so that greater or smaller deviations could be decided by the school. The rules regarding teachers' working hours which are laid down through negotiations with the central teachers' organisations were furthermore made more flexible, so that the school, to a greater extent, may decide how to utilise the working hours of the individual teacher.

The financing of the schools

The vocational education and training reform established a new grant system based on the "taximeter" principles. The grant is divided into a grant towards expenses related directly to the teaching and a grant towards expenses not directly related to the activity. Grants directly related to the teaching are awarded according to the "taximeter" system, *i.e.* a grant is awarded per student. The "taximeter" consists of two parts: an objective activity target and a rate.

The activity target is student full-time equivalents. A student full-time equivalent is the designation of 40 student-weeks, in which the student spends his whole weekly workload on school work (including homework).

The rate is the amount of the grant awarded per student full-time equivalent. The rate is laid down in the annual appropriation acts for large groups of courses. The courses are divided into groups on the basis of the expenditure needs of the courses in order to be able to carry out the teaching, and each group has one "taximeter" rate. The expenses which are directly related to the teaching comprises four elements:

- teacher salaries;
- salaries for other staff assisting in the implementation of the teaching (*e.g.* workshop assistants);
- expenses relating to the provision of materials, textbooks/teaching aids, etc.;
- expenses relating to the acquisition of apparatus (equipment).

The division of courses into groups is based on general objective criteria, and these criteria have been laid down by the Minister on the recommendation of the Council for Vocational Education. The duration of the courses is laid down in the individual education orders, so that the computation of student full-time equivalents is objective and comparable.

The rates laid down in the Appropriation Act reflect political decisions regarding the economic standard, and the schools must adapt their organisation of the courses to this economic standard which is laid down by the politicians. The grant is adjusted on a regular basis in relation to the actual number of student full-time equivalents. The grant is thus rapidly adapted to the actual activity.

In the field of vocational education and training different "taximeter" rates were applied in 1992 ranging from 8 000 DKr (open education — the Merkonom modular study programme) to 60 000 DKr (further technical courses, rate 4).

- Grants towards joint expenses

The joint expenses comprise the expenses relating to:

- rent and mortgage interests (capital expenditure),
- operation of buildings,
- management and administration,
- various other expenses which are common to the school.

The grant is a framework grant by which is understood that the grant framework laid down in the Appropriation Act is decisive for the size of the grant, and that there is no regular adjustment of the grant in relation to the actual number of student full-time equivalents during the individual fiscal year. The computation is thus made once a year at the beginning of the fiscal year based on the number of student full-time equivalents of the previous year.

The joint expense model divides the grant into the following elements:

- basic grants and supplements to basic grants per school,
- grants dependent on student full-time equivalents towards the joint expenses,
- adjustment in relation to seniority, age reduction and local allowance,
- grants towards rent, mortgage interests, taxes and excises.

- Basic grants towards joint expenses per school

Joint expenses (for management and administration) is computed on the basis of fixed rates for basic grants per school as well as rates and guidelines for the distribution of supplements to the individual school, *e.g.* due to the type of school (commercial or technical school), certain courses/educational areas or other criteria. The basic grant amounts to 730 000 DKr for commercial schools and 1 210 000 DKr for technical schools.

- Grant towards joint expenses dependent on the number of student full-time equivalents

A supplement towards the joint expenses is computed on the basis of the number of student full-time equivalents per school of the previous fiscal year. This grant towards the joint expenses in relation to management, administration and the operation of buildings is computed on the basis of the number of student full-time equivalents and a rate per student full-time equivalent as well as a rate per prescribed area per student full-time equivalent, respectively. In connection with the computations relating to the operation of buildings, all courses have been ascribed an area norm. Four standard norms are used which comprise 90 per cent of the courses.

The administration rate amounts to 2 600 DKr per student full-time equivalent enrolled in commercial courses, and to 4 000 DKr per student full-time equivalent enrolled in technical courses.

- Grants towards capital expenses

As a point of departure, the grant comprises all expenses relating to rent, irrespective of whether they relate to rent contracts or mortgage interests in connection with the school's own buildings. Adjustments are subsequently made on the basis of the relationship between the actual area consumption and the prescribed area consumption. The prescribed area consumption is computed on the basis of the number of student full-time equivalents per course in the previous year multiplied by the prescribed area per student per course. This prescribed area is compared with the actual area consumption of the school. The difference between the actual and prescribed areas is multiplied by the annually fixed rate per square meter. One then arrives at the amount with which the actual rent expenses are to be adjusted.

- The total grant is awarded as a block grant

The school can decide how to utilise the grants awarded, irrespective of whether they are "taximeter" grants towards expenses directly related to the teaching or they are framework grants towards the joint expenses. It is however a condition that the regulations laid down at central level with regard to the individual courses are complied with, and that the number of student full-time equivalents on which the "taximeter" grant rests is correct.

- Other grants

A number of pool grant systems have furthermore been established from which schools can apply for grants for special purposes.

Teacher qualifications and teacher training

The teaching staff at the vocational schools is characterised by a variety of different qualifications.

In order to be appointed, the teacher must either have a vocational education and training background within one or several relevant training areas supplemented by a relevant qualification acquired in further or higher technical or commercial education or another relevant further education qualification.

Apart from this, relevant and topical vocational experience — five years — is required for teachers who are to teach in the directly occupationally-oriented vocational areas, and two years for other teachers. Furthermore, the teacher should possess or have acquired — at the latest two years after his appointment — a broad general background corresponding to the level of the subjects taught in the general subject range of the vocational upper secondary school within the relevant area.

Within the first two years, the teacher must also have acquired a pedagogical or subject-related/pedagogical qualification corresponding to the level of the pedagogical basic courses carried out at the State Institute for the Educational Training of Vocational Teachers (SEL).

Assessment of vocational education

All courses at the vocational schools are subject to a continuous external assessment of the efficiency of the system by virtue of the close relationship to the users of the system.

This is in particular reflected in the vocational education and training programmes, where the Council for Vocational Education and the trade committees continuously monitor and have the overall responsibility for the relevance of the content of the courses. To this should be added that major review and analysis work is organised on a regular basis with a view to assuring the quality and efficiency of the courses.

Problems in vocational education

Throughout the 1980s, the vocational education system has been faced with a considerable shortage of practical training places, and many students have therefore been unable to complete their training programmes.

The situation upon completion of the basic year of basic vocational education (EFG) and — as of 1991 — of the second school period is illustrated in Figure 6.

For 1984, 1988 and 1992 the proportional distribution of the students is indicated. The figures for 1992 comprise only the first 6 months.

It should be added that Figure 6 only illustrates the situation for those starting their training course directly at a vocational school.

Figure 6. **The practical training situation for the cohorts having completed the EFG basic year/2nd school period in June of the period 1984-1992**
Calculated as per 1 December

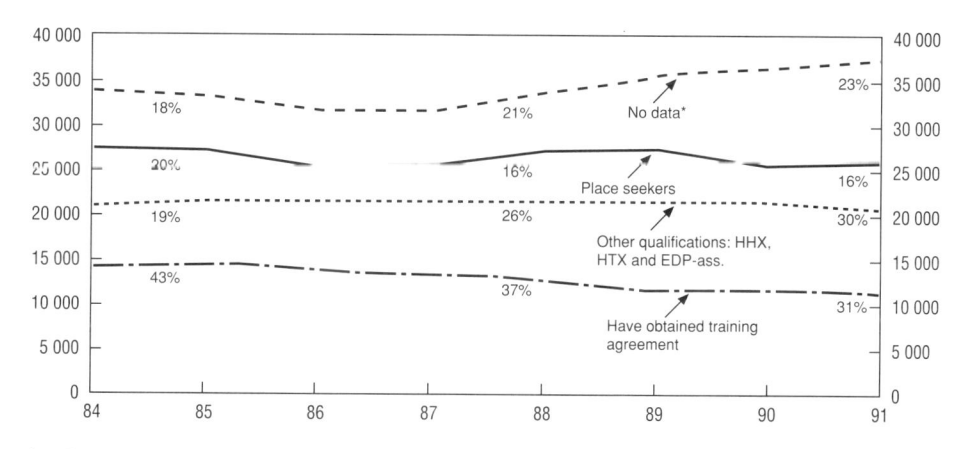

[Chart showing four curves from 1984 to 1991:
- Total students (top curve): 18% (1984), 21% (1988), 23% (1991) — No data*
- Place seekers: 20% (1984), 16% (1988), 16% (1991)
- Other qualifications: HHX, HTX and EDP-ass.: 19% (1984), 26% (1988), 30% (1991)
- Have obtained training agreement: 43% (1984), 37% (1988), 31% (1991)]

* Partly based on estimate.
Source: Danish Ministry of Education (1994), *Danish Youth Education, Problems and Achievements*.

The upper curve indicates the total number of students having completed the EFG basic year/second school period. The figure also shows the number of students from a cohort having secured a practical training place within six months of completion, the number having entered education programmes for Higher Commercial Examination (HHX), Higher Technical Examination (HTX) or EDP Assistant, or those registered as seeking traineeships, finally, the number of students not belonging to any of these groups. A large number of these students do not complete their training course.

The general trend is a decreasing number of students continuing their training with a training agreement. At the same time a growing number continue on an alternative programme, primarily HHX and HTX. In spite of the fact that cohorts have increase by approximately 4 000 students, the number of students securing a training agreement has dropped by approximately 2 000. The proportion of the cohorts having secured a practical training place has dropped from 43 per cent in 1984 to 24 per cent in 1992.

On this background a scheme was introduced in June 1990, establishing a school-based practical training programme for students who were not able to get a regular practical training place. This scheme, however, has not fulfilled the expectations in terms of constituting a real guarantee for students without a regular practical training place. The first intake for school-based practical training in January 1991 counted 1 900 students only, out of a total of 4 100 place-seekers, in the second year, a year later, the figure was 2 400 out of 6 000, and in the third year, in the spring of 1992, the figure was 400 out of 1 400. This amounted to 46 per cent, 40 per cent and 29 per cent of the place-seekers respectively.

Following this the Parliament adopted in 1992 a subsidy scheme impelling the business enterprises to take trainees. The subsidy scheme involves both the public and the private sectors. The main elements of the scheme are:

— Granting of direct subsidies to employers who create trainee places. Typically, the total subsidy amounts to DKr 52 000, *i.e.* DKr 20 000 in the first year (1993) and DKr 16 000 in the subsequent two years. The subsidy applies to all training agreements concluded since 1 August 1992.
— Greater responsibility to the vocational schools. In future, the schools are responsible for the school-based training programme. The principal aim is to procure regular practical training places for the students, but failing that, to offer school-based practical training course.
— The scheme is financed by contributions from public as well as private employers which amounted to DKr 1 500 per employee in 1993. The size of the contributions is fixed on an annual basis.

Other vocationally-oriented or semiprofessional types of education for young people

Agricultural education

The Danish agricultural schools were established during the last decades of the 19th century, *i.e.* during the same period during which the folk high school movement became an important cultural factor in Denmark.

For almost a century, the folk high schools and the agricultural schools were more or less alike. And it was not until the 1960s that the latter developed into purely vocational schools and in 1989 the "sandwich-principle" was introduced.

The basic social and health training programmes

It is the aim of these courses to qualify staff in the welfare, health care and nursing areas for broad-based functions, so that patients and clients do not have to deal with so many different staff groups, when they find themselves in a situation where they need to make use of the care and welfare services.

The training system comprises long practical training periods within the work area in question and theoretical instruction at a school and is structured in phases as a co-ordinated system with three qualification levels:

- a one-year basic training programme for social and health service helps,
- a 1½-year advanced training programme for social and health service assistants,
- further education courses leading to qualifications in nursing, socio-educational work, etc.

Home economics education

There are approximately 25 home economics schools in Denmark. They are state subsidized free independent schools for young people above 16 years of age.

The teaching consists of general information with the emphasis laid on health and society, family and housekeeping. The course duration vary between one week and one year. The offer of the schools is very varied, as the individual school creates its own profile through, for instance, offers of sport activities, handicraft or "children in the family".

The kitchen assistant's course, which is a vocational education and training course, also takes place at the home economics schools and is of a duration of two years, including periods of practical training.

It is also possible to be trained as a matron at the home economics schools. The course is of three years' duration, of which 40 weeks take place at school.

Maritime education

The maritime education courses are managed by the Ministry of Industry, Commerce, Trade and Shipping and comprise the following:
- The Ship's Assistant's (able-bodied seaman) Course is organised as an 26-month alternance course, where school periods alternate with practical training periods on board.
- The Navigation Courses of 6-36-month duration for coastal skippers, masters of fishing vessels, officers of the watch, home-trade masters and shipmasters.
- The Marine Engineering Course for skilled iron- and metal-workers is organised as day school of three years' duration.
- The Ship's Cook's Course is a 5-week course for skilled cooks.

The civil services' education

• Assistant in the postal services and the state railways

The courses are of two years' duration and alternate between theoretical education and practical training. In order to be admitted to the course, trainees must be 18 years of age, Danish nationals and in perfect health.

- The state tax and administration course

The course, which is of four years' duration, is a "sandwich" course where theoretical education alternates with practical training. Trainees are employed as heads of section in customs and tax and receive approximately 20 weeks of theoretical education each year at the Tax and Administration School. In order to be employed as heads of section in customs and tax and commence on the course, trainees must have completed one of the following courses: the HHX, the upper secondary school leaving examination, the HF or a similar course.

Company education (banks, insurance companies, etc.)

Insurance companies train their own staff to become insurance agents. The courses take place partly in an insurance company partly at the Insurance School. The course shall be completed and the examination passed at the latest four years after employment. Also the banks do train to a certain extent their own staff to assume certain functions.

Upper Secondary Education

Upper secondary education is offered in different forms and at different types of institutions. General upper secondary education is offered at general upper secondary schools (*Gymnasium*) or courses preparing for the upper secondary leaving examination (*Studentereksamen*) and the courses for the Higher Preparatory Examination (HF), while the commercial and technical schools offer courses for the Higher Commercial Examination (HHX) and the Higher Technical Examination (HTX) respectively.

The Gymnasium and the courses for the upper secondary leaving examination (Studentereksamenskurser)

The *Gymnasium* has its origin in the cathedral and monastery schools established by the Catholic Church in the early Middle Ages and seven of the schools established in the 12th and 13th centuries are still in existence today.

During the second half of this century the number of upper secondary schools has doubled. The present number is 141. One of these is a state school. Eighteen are state-subsidised private schools and the rest is county schools.

At present the upper secondary schools and the two years' courses for the *Studentereksamen* are regulated by the Act of 13 June 1990 on Upper Secondary Schools and Courses. According to the act the aim of the *Gymnasium* and the two-years' courses is to provide a general education as well as to prepare the students for continued studies.

Admission rules

Schools applicants must have completed nine or ten years of basic education, including English from the 5th form and a second foreign language from the 7th form (German or French). The school of origin must declare the applicant qualified for the *Gymnasium*, and applicants must have taken the Leaving Examination of the *Folkeskole* with satisfactory results in Danish and mathematics and — for applicants to the languages line — in English, German or French, or — for applicants to the mathematics line — in science.

Courses applicants must have completed ten years of basic education, including English from the 5th form, and a second foreign language from the 7th form (German or French). For applicants coming directly from the *Folkeskole*, the school of origin must declare the applicant qualified for upper secondary education, and applicants must have taken the Advanced Leaving Examination of the *Folkeskole* with satisfactory results. For other applicants, the headmaster of the course shall consider the applicant qualified.

The structure and content of the upper secondary school

The course of instruction at the upper secondary school lasts three years and is given in two different lines, the languages line and the mathematics line. Instruction comprises obligatory subjects, common to all students in the line chosen and optional subjects. Optional subjects shall be on two levels: high and intermediate levels.

The obligatory subjects in both lines are biology, classical studies, religious education, Danish, English, geography, history, music, visual arts and physical education and sports.

In the languages line instruction also includes German or French at continuation level, German, French, Italian, Japanese, Spanish or Russian at beginner's level as well as Latin and natural science (mathematics/physics/chemistry).

In the mathematics line the instruction also includes chemistry, mathematics and physics as well as French or German at continuation level or German, French, Spanish, Italian, or Russian at beginner's level.

The high level optional subjects are English and German at continuation and at beginner's levels Spanish, Italian, Japanese, Russian, Latin, Greek, social studies, biology, chemistry, physics, mathematics and music. Latin and Greek may only be chosen by students in the languages line. Physics and chemistry may only be chosen by students in the mathematics line. English is organised differently as between the two lines.

The intermediate level optional subjects are biology, business, economics, chemistry, computer science, design, drama, film and TV studies, geography, Latin, mathematics, music, philosophy, psychology, physical education and sport, physics, social studies, technical studies and visual arts. Mathematics and physics may only be chosen by students in the languages line. Chemistry and Latin are organised differently as between the two lines. The Ministry of Education may approve the offering of instruction in other optional subjects than those named.

Regarding the content of instruction in the individual subjects the Minister of Education has issued a special executive order on subjects.

The instruction also includes a major written assignment in the 3rd form in Danish, history or one of the student's optional subjects at the high level. All students also receive instruction in electronic data processing.

For the single student, instruction comprises the obligatory subjects, and optional subjects to the number of four or five weekly lessons in the second form and 14 or 15 weekly lessons in the third form. The major written assignment shall be in addition to this. A subject may only be chosen at one level and the same subject at intermediate level may not be chosen in both the second and the third forms.

Students in the languages line must choose at least one language at the high level and students in the mathematics line must choose one out of mathematics, physics, chemistry, biology, music and social studies at the high level. Those who choose both Latin and Greek as optional subjects at the high level shall complete instruction in their continuation language or beginner's language after the first form, at their own choice. Students who choose Greek at the high level will not participate in instruction in classical studies in the third form.

Students in the mathematics line who choose either social studies or music at the high level shall further choose at least one of the following subjects: mathematics at the high level, physics at the high level, biology at the intermediate level, geography at the intermediate level or chemistry at the intermediate level.

The choice of French, Italian, Japanese, Russian, Spanish or German as optional subject presupposes that the student has received instruction in the language(s) concerned in the first and second forms of the upper secondary school. The school year consists of 199 days including the examination period.

Internal evaluation

The aim of the continuous evaluation is to guide the student and the teacher with a view to the further planning of the instruction. The teacher shall follow the benefits gained from the instruction by the single student as well as by the whole class. At suitable intervals, this shall be discussed collectively and individually with the students. The whole course of instruction shall be evaluated by means of tests, special assignments/reports or conversations.

External evaluation

Evaluation of the individual student's qualifications in the subject shall also be made for external purposes. This shall be done by means of the following forms of evaluation: marks for the year's work, examination marks, term marks and testimonials.

Marks for the year's work, which are to appear on the student's examination certificate, shall be given at the end of the school year in which instruction in the subject concerned is concluded. Marks for the year's work are given by the teacher of the subject concerned and express the judgement of the latter on the student's level of attainment at the end of the year.

Term marks shall be given in those subjects in which marks for the year's work are given. Term marks shall be given twice during the school year and, in the case of subjects which are to be continued in the following year, also at the end of the school year. These marks may be accompanied by a written testimonial as to the student's aptitude for, and work with, the subject concerned.

The upper secondary school leaving examination — written and oral examinations

A total of ten examinations must be taken in order to pass the complete examination, of which up to three may be taken after the first and the second years.

After the third year, all students take a written examination in Danish and in the subjects chosen at the high level. The number of oral examinations varies for the individual student in accordance with the number of subjects chosen at high level.

Written examinations are based on national question papers, produced by the Ministry's Department of Upper Secondary Education. For each subject, there is an examination committee consisting of hand-picked teachers and the Department's consultant(s) for the subject in question. Oral examinations take place in the subjects selected (at random) by the Department of Upper Secondary Education for each individual school. By the end of April all subject consultants must have accepted all "petita" (lists of texts, etc., offered by individual classes for the oral examination).

For each subject, there is a permanent group of external examiners made up by teachers — with 5 per cent members from other sectors of the education system or from industry.

Written examination papers are marked by two external examiners, *i.e.* the teacher has no share in the mark given, but is given two days to ask for a reconsideration of individual marks. The examiners may alter the mark under the impression of the teacher's arguments, or decide to stick to their original result.

At oral examinations, the teacher and one external examiner together decide the mark. In case of disagreement between two neighbouring figures on the marking scale, the external examiner has the last word.

Students are given a mark (scale from 0 to 13) for the year's work as well as for their achievement at the examinations. The average of the two sets of marks is then the pupil's "examination result". In order to pass, the student must have an average of minimum 6.0.

The courses

The upper secondary school leaving examination can be taken as a full examination following a two-year course. Examination may also be taken following study at single-subject course. Examinations in single subjects can be pieced together to form a complete upper secondary school leaving examination.

Like at the upper secondary school complete upper secondary school leaving examination may be taken at a course in one of two lines: the languages line and the mathematics line and include obligatory subjects, common to all students in the chosen line, and optional subjects, which may be chosen by students of both lines. Optional subjects are to be offered at two levels, high and intermediate. At the courses the instruction is given in a more concentrated form and music, visual arts and physical education and sports are not obligatory subjects.

Higher preparatory examination course (HF)

Background

The Higher Preparatory Examination (HF) was introduced in 1967 in a political climate of extending educational possibilities to new groups of society. Originally the idea was to create a two-year course aimed specifically at prospective candidates for teacher training. There was, however, concern that this concept might result in an educational "cul-de-sac". So the course design was changed into an alternative route to further and higher education, *formally* (though it has to be said not always *in reality*) equivalent to the existing three-year course leading to the *Studentereksamen*.

HF is the "sweeper" of the general upper secondary education level. In the *Gymnasium*, there is (still) an overrepresentation of middle class children (50 per cent male / 50 per cent female), whereas HF recruits its predominantly female students from a broader base of society. Two-year HF courses are established at 77 different places in the country — mostly at upper secondary schools and teacher training colleges, although a small number of independent HF-institutions also exist. In addition to that the 60 adult education centres (VUC) *inter alia* offer single subject HF-instruction as well as single subject upper secondary school instruction.

Today the HF courses come under the Act of 13 June 1990 on Higher Preparatory Examination Courses and on Single-Subject Courses Preparatory to Further Studies for adults.

Admission rules

Applicants must have finished lower secondary education at least one year before admission to the course and must be accepted by the HF institution as qualified. Applicants wishing to be admitted directly from lower secondary school to a two-year course must have completed ten years of primary and lower secondary education and must be considered qualified by their schools of origin.

Course structure and content

The Higher Preparatory Examination can be taken as a complete examination after a two-year course comprising common core subjects, three optional subjects and a major written assignment. It can also be taken following single-subject instruction. Examinations in the single subjects can be pieced together into a complete higher preparatory examination. The teaching year consists of 199 days including the examination period.

Written and oral examinations

HF examinations are administered in the same way as the *Studentereksamen*. With the new credit transfer system, certain levels are now marked together with the equivalent *Studentereksamen* subject by the same group of external examiners. An important difference from the *Studentereksamen* is that a complete HF examination requires an oral and/or written examination in every subject studied.

Like the *Studentereksamen*, the HF gives admission to further and higher education although specific optional subjects or a specific level of attainment normally will be required.

Teacher qualifications and assessment of teachers

Teachers at upper secondary schools and courses all have a Master's degree — normally in a major and a minor subjects. Before permanent engagement can be obtained the student teacher must go through a course for the diploma in education. The course should normally be taken during the first of the two years when he or she is engaged on probation. The theoretical part is given in classes established at regional level and is finished with a written examination. The practical part takes place at a school or a course under the guidance of an experienced teacher in each of the student teacher's subject and comprises 120 lessons as a minimum. At the end of the practical part the guiding teacher, the leader of the courses in education and the subject consultant of the Ministry attend the student teacher's teaching in at least two lessons. After that a written statement on the teaching abilities of the student teacher is issued.

There is general confidence in the examination system of the schools as a safeguard of quality and "standards", and there is general confidence that the teachers themselves guard the quality, for example through their professional environment.

The upper secondary schools — and courses — are regularly visited by subject consultants from the Ministry of Education who attend lessons in their subject and give the teachers advice if necessary. If a headmaster gets the impression that the quality of the teacher's work is lacking behind he or she should call upon the subject consultant(s) who will attend a number of the teacher's lessons and advise him or her on how to improve the quality of the teaching. After a couple of months the consultant will return to see whether the situation has improved. If not the teacher may be dismissed.

As mentioned previously external examiners take part in the written and oral examinations of the upper secondary schools and courses. If the achievements of the students in general are too poor, the external examiner will report to the headmaster and to the Department for Upper Secondary Education and action may be taken against the teacher.

Local government of upper secondary schools and courses

The county council

— establishes, runs and closes down schools and courses and ensures that schools and courses have a capacity big enough to admit all qualified applicants;
— fixes the grants for the operational expenses and investments of the schools and the extent of special education;
— appoints the headmaster after having obtained the opinion of the Ministry on the qualifications of the applicants and appoints and dismisses teachers and other members of staff on the recommendation of the headmaster;
— fixes the maximum number of classes of the school/course and the minimum number of students which the school/course is bound to admit;
— fixes the statutes of the school/course.

The county council may direct the school/course to offer certain optional subjects. Finally, the council is the instance of appeal for decisions made by the boards of the schools and courses.

The School and Course Boards

They consist of:

— representatives of the county council and the municipal councils of the catchment area;
— representatives of the parents (at schools only);
— representatives of the staff and the students (who cannot form the majority of the board).

Other interested parties, for instance local business, may be represented in the board, if there is a special need for it. The headmaster takes part in the board meetings without the right to vote.

The board

— fixes, apart from the salaries, on the recommendation of the headmaster the distribution of the budget frame fixed by the county council on the different accounts of the school/course;
— fixes the maximum number of students per class;

— fixes on the recommendation of the headmaster the number of non-obligatory subjects;
— fixes the holiday-plan of the school/course;
— fixes the rules of order of the school/course.

The headmaster

He/she is the pedagogical and administrative leader of the school and the local representative of the central pedagogical authority — the Ministry of Education. He/she is responsible for the teaching and examinations and the issue of examination certificates.

As pedagogical leader the headmaster decides *inter alia* on the following matters:

— the annual allocation of subjects and lessons among the teachers;
— the allocation of other tasks among the staff;
— non-obligatory subjects to be taught;
— the admission of students;
— all individual matters concerning the students, including expulsion of students.

Complaints against the headmaster's pedagogical decisions are to be brought before the Minister of Education.

As administrative leader the headmaster is responsible to the county council for the running of the school/course and to the board for the matters coming under the competence of the board. Furthermore the headmaster is responsible for the running and maintenance of the school buildings. Finally the headmaster makes the decision on all matters where other authorities do not have the competence.

The Pedagogical Council

It consists of the headmaster and all the teachers of the school/course. The Pedagogical Council is the headmaster's advisory body. Typical items for consultation are the subjects to be offered by the school/course, the allocation of subjects and lessons, excursion guidelines, experiments, theme-days and study circles.

The Student Council

It submits statements to the headmaster, who may discuss the subjects to be offered by the school/course, the allocation of subjects and lessons, excursion guidelines, experiments, theme-days and study circles with the council. The relation between the teaching and the work load of the students may also be discussed. The council cannot, however, comment on individual teachers' conditions.

Higher commercial examination and higher technical examination courses

The history of the courses

The present courses leading to the Higher Commercial Examination (HHX) and the Higher Technical Examination (HTX) build on an act from 1990. This act made it possible for qualified students to go directly from the basic school to a 3-year (HHX) or a 2^1/$_2$-3-year (HTX) course, of which the last two years are spent on the actual upper secondary course. At the same time, a division of all subjects into levels created a greater comparability with the general upper secondary school. The academic aim was furthermore strengthened.

The higher commercial examination

The HHX was started in 1888 on private initiative at Niels Brock's Commercial School in Copenhagen with a structure which in the main can be found in the course today. The range of subjects comprised both commercial and general subjects.

It was not until 1972 that the HHX was given the status of a university entrance examination in connection with a revision of the contents and the introduction of more rigorous admission requirements. At the beginning of the 1970s, the course was run by almost half of the Danish commercial schools, and just under 2 000 students graduated from the two-year course and almost 1 000 from the one-year course. The one-year course started as early as in 1917, when it was reserved for those who — after having passed the *Studentereksamen* — were not interested in higher education. The one-year course still exists.

As of 1982, the course was offered at all commercial schools, and the intake has now reached approximately 10 000 students a year.

Higher technical examination

The HTX-course was established on an experimental basis in 1982. The reason for its establishment was a desire to contribute to a broader supply of education and training possibilities following the EFG-basic courses and a desire to create a new and relevant way of access to higher education in the technical area. In this context, it was of importance that fewer and fewer skilled workers continued at the engineering colleges (*teknika*) whereas the number of upper secondary graduates increased significantly.

The pilot period lasted until the spring of 1988, after which the programme was evaluated and made permanent after minor adjustments of the individual subjects. On the same occasion, the HTX-course was granted the status of a qualifying examination and the graduates were now in principle placed on an equal footing with the *Gymnasium*, HF and HHX as far as access to higher education was concerned.

Today, the HTX-course consists of a vocational education part of $^1/_2$-1 years' duration followed by a two-year vocational upper secondary education part. The course aims at further studies particularly of a technical nature and consists of technological subjects including workshop instruction, natural sciences subjects, language subjects including Danish, and social science subjects. The central subjects of the course have a level which corresponds to that of the intermediate level of the *Gymnasium*. Among the optional subjects of the course, which comprise approximately 1/3 of the time of study, the students must choose at least two subjects at the highest upper secondary level. In the second year of the HTX-course, the course is divided into a building technology, a mechanical, an electrical and a process-technical line. The course is organised with a relatively heavy emphasis on technical topics which are often used as a point of departure for the theory in *e.g.* the natural sciences subjects. Upon completion of a practical training period in a firm, young people with an HTX-examination meet both the theoretical and general as well as vocational requirements for entry to the advanced technician's courses and the engineering colleges. Like the HHX, the HTX at the same time qualifies for admission to the other higher education institutions.

In 1992, approximately 2 500 students were admitted, of which around 10 per cent were girls.

Admission requirements

There are two ways of entering a vocational upper secondary programme — either directly after the *Folkeskole* or on completion of one year of a vocational education and training course at a commercial school or $^1/_2$-1 year at a technical school. In order to be admitted, a student must be considered qualified by the vocational school, and as far as the HHX is concerned the student must furthermore meet a number of specific requirements, in particular with regard to foreign language skills. In both cases, the vocational education and training year is shared by the students who want a vocational education and training qualification and the students who want a vocational upper secondary qualification.

At the end of the basic 6 months/1 year, the vocational school assesses whether the student is qualified to continue to the vocational upper secondary programme. The assessment of the school includes the student's maturity, independence and the results obtained in the basic course.

For the HHX course, it is required that the students have a good knowledge of English and of a second foreign language or mathematics.

The HTX-course is in particular based on knowledge in Danish, mathematics, physics (science) and foreign languages. To this should be added experience from a workshop-related subject. Approximately 2/3 of the course consist of obligatory subjects, and approximately 1/3 of optional subjects.

The Ministry each year decides which examinations are to be held. Each student shall normally take part in a minimum of ten and a maximum of twelve examinations.

The upper secondary education credit transfer system

In connection with the implementation of the new legislation on the *Gymnasium* and HF the Minister of Education issued an executive order on credit transfer between the different types of upper secondary education including the Greenland upper secondary education.

The main rule is that a student is exempted from instruction and examination in a subject, in which he or she already has passed the examination with the mark 6 as a minimum at the same or a higher level at one of the other types of upper secondary education. The mark previously obtained is transferred to the new examination certificate. In addition to that the headmaster may exempt a student from instruction and examination in a subject, in which he or she has passed an examination at the same or a higher level at an other education than upper secondary education. In this case the mark is, however, not transferred to the new certificate.

All relevant subjects taught in the different types of upper secondary education have been divided into three levels: A (high level), B (intermediate level) and C (lower level).

Each subject has been placed at the different levels according to a concrete assessment based upon the following elements: the total number of lessons, the requirements of the student's foundation in the subject, the immersion in the subject, whether a written examination is held, and demand on the teacher's qualifications. This means that a subject taught at two types of upper secondary education can be placed at the same level, although the exact professional content of the subject may vary.

The central government of upper secondary education

The Danish Parliament lays down the overall targets and framework for the upper secondary level, including the *Gymnasium*, HF, HHX and HTX.

The Ministry of Education issues curriculum and examination regulations. For the HTX and the HHX, guidelines are issued by advisory bodies, on which employee and employer representatives form the majority.

Aims, syllabus and examination form for each subject are laid down at central level. Room has however been made for schools and teachers to decide on the actual content of the teaching. The Ministry of Education is responsible for controlling the quality of education. The management of the individual educational institutions enjoy a high degree of real autonomy, and central control focuses its attention on the quality of the work through quality development projects, examination papers drawn up at central level, and general guidelines in written form and through advisory functions.

Complaints are always addressed to the educational institutions in question, and problems are usually solved at local level. The Ministry is only involved, when this is not the case. Complaints concerning admission cannot be brought before the Ministry.

The quality development project in upper secondary education

The main aims of general upper secondary education are to provide general education and to prepare the students for continued studies. In order to measure whether these aims are attained a number of indicators have to be identified and used.

Statistical indicators represent exact instruments of measurement. The following indicators which are more difficult to measure exactly are, however, an important part of the evaluation if one has to have a full picture of the quality of education:

— have the students matured?
— have they gained independence?
— have they achieved relevant learning have they got insight through the study of different subjects and do they find a coherence in their studies?
— are they well-equipped to become active citizens?
— have they understood something about scientific methods?
— have they developed an attitude to culture?
— can they relate to world-wide problems?

Evaluation of institutions

The evaluation team spends four days at the school and examines the following issues:

The teaching: attending as many lessons as possible they observe:

— the teacher performance (plan, handling, personality);
— the teaching methods and their relevance;
— the performance and active participation of the students (there is a strong oral tradition in Danish teaching);
— the content and its correspondence with the curriculum.

The management and its:

— strategies;
— planning;
— administrative methods;
— delegating ability;
— ability to develop and initiate;
— support to staff and students;
— co-operation ability.

The administration and its:

— effectiveness;
— service to students, teachers and other interested parties;
— communication and ways of information;
— ability to co-operate.

The students and their:

— active participation in the life of the school;
— attitude towards the school (interviews);
— future plans.

Ways of co-operation:

— school board;
— staff council;
— committee work (participation);
— subject committees;
— co-operation between colleagues (support/supervision);
— extra-curricular activities;
— interplay between the school and its partners — the role of the school in the local community;
— buildings and equipment.

All these elements of the school are analysed, evaluated and described in a report. The report contains descriptions, emphasises strong and weak sides of the school and gives advice for ways of improving and changing. On the basis of the report, the school works out an action programme. After a year the evaluation team returns to the school for a one-day visit, to ascertain the amount of change and improvement.

Self-evaluation

For some years the Ministry has been working together with 14 schools on a project of self-evaluation. The result of this has been published in a pamphlet about different methods of carrying through a self-evaluation project. This pamphlet has also been distributed to all upper secondary institutions for inspiration.

The transition from upper secondary education to short, medium and long higher education

General qualifications

The following examinations qualify for admission to higher education: 1) *Studentereksamen*, 2) HF, 3) HHX and 4) HTX; furthermore Upper Secondary Absorption Courses for Refugees (*Gymnasiale indslusningskurser for flygtninge*, GIF) have been introduced. HTX and especially GIF form only a small contingent to the total amount of candidates who apply for admission to higher education.

Special qualifications

Possessing one of the general qualification examinations does not necessarily give sufficient qualifications for attending a course at university level.

Special qualifications take effect under two different forms: some are specific admission requirements that have to be fulfilled before admission; others are so called "study start" requirements. The study start requirements are not conditions for admission; they mark, however, the previous knowledge that the students are required to possess at the beginning of the course.

The first type of special admission requirements occurs for example when a student with a *Studentereksamen* of predominantly language-type wishes to enter a course in one of the natural sciences; it is then required that the student in addition passes an examination in one or more specially designed, preparatory natural science subjects before he/she can obtain admission.

The second type of special qualifications required (the "study start" requirements) occurs for example when a student with a mathematical upper secondary school leaving examination wishes to study theology or classical philology. The student must qualify in Latin and Greek and in this case it can be done after admission has taken place.

However, as part of the 4-year plan (1993-96) that the Minister of Education and parties of the Opposition agreed upon in June 1992 this scheme will be reformed in such a way that admission qualification requirements for every field of higher education will include "study-start" qualification requirements. The new scheme will take effect in 1995.

The admission regulation system

Most higher education courses come according to the Act on Admission Regulation of 16 May 1990 under the Co-ordinated Application Scheme (*Den Koordinerede Tilmelding*, KOT). Admission to higher education is always decided by the institution concerned as admission is decentralised to the institutions. But the technical management is data-processed and centrally co-ordinated by the KOT Agency. The idea of the scheme is that students can apply for more than one course at the same time in order of priority, but can be admitted to only one of the courses (highest possible priority).

The main features of the present (1992) system

Study places are as a rule divided into two quotas. For the Advanced Technical Courses and certain other courses admission is only through Quota 2.

Quota 1: Study places are allocated to the candidates in order of falling average marks in the Upper Secondary examinations mentioned earlier.

Quota 2: The following groups of candidates come into consideration:

— Candidates who have a qualifying examination (according to Quota 1) and who in addition fulfil the criteria defined by the institution for each course or each admission area.

— Candidates who have received exemption from the requirement of a qualifying examination, and who in the view of the receiving institution possess knowledge and experience of a nature which makes it probable that they will be able to complete the course applied for.
— Candidates who have completed another course of higher education of at least three years' duration.
— Candidates with a foreign examination equivalent to a Danish qualifying examination.

Quota 2 gives each institution the authority to determine the qualification criteria it finds most suitable. This is a real change as Quota 2 contains about one half of the total number of candidates. This scheme will continue to be in effect until 1995; at that time admission as a whole will have been transferred to the institutions who then may alter and develop the system according to their wishes.

Table 12 indicates the proportion of young people who, after general upper secondary education, continue in vocational education or higher education.

Alternative and Supplementary Education and Training for the 14-18-Year-Olds

Continuation schools (Efterskoler)

The continuation schools are approved and economically supported by the State. To obtain State approval and support a continuation school must meet the following requirements:
— The schools must be a private, self-governing boarding school offering general education to pupils 14-18 years of age.
— The headmaster must be approved by the Ministry of Education.
— The curriculum of the school must be approved by the Ministry of Education.

The Ministry approves any curriculum plan ensuring that the pupils get a general (liberal) education and will not interfere when schools give their curricula a special pedagogical, religious or political profile. One should, however, bear in mind that most continuation schools prepare their students for the same final examinations as the *Folkeskole* and that this to some extent limits the amount of curricular-freedom exercised.

Continuation schools with special emphasis on special education and practical work represent especially a second chance for late developed and non-intellectually gifted pupils who have suffered defeat in the ordinary school-system. Several of these schools use the practical work to build up the self-confidence of the pupils and to motivate them to learn and understand the theory necessary to solve the problems stemming from the practical work.

When a continuation school is approved it is entitled to a State support covering 50-85 per cent of the costs connected with the educational activities. The total State support amounted in 1992 to 769 million DKr corresponding to 38 200 DKr per pupil.

Table 12. **Proportion of young people, who after general upper secondary education continue in vocational education or higher education distributed, by sex, 1981/82 - 1990/91**

	81/82	82/83	83/84	84/85	85/86	86/87	87/88	88/89	89/90	90/91
All	85	86	86	86	86	87	87	87	89	90
Vocational education	27	28	29	30	30	28	27	29	26	27
of which: higher comm. ex.	8	8	7	7	7	6	6	7	6	6
Higher education	58	57	57	56	55	59	60	58	62	63
Short-cycle	7	7	4	4	4	4	3	3	5	6
Medium-cycle	32	31	34	36	36	37	37	38	39	39
Long-cycle	18	19	19	16	16	17	19	17	18	18
Men	86	86	87	86	86	86	86	87	88	90
Vocational education	30	29	29	28	28	26	25	27	26	26
of which: higher comm. ex.	9	7	6	6	5	5	5	6	6	5
Higher education	56	57	58	58	58	60	62	60	62	64
Short-cycle	4	4	3	3	3	4	3	3	4	6
Medium-cycle	29	28	30	33	34	34	34	35	34	34
Long-cycle	23	25	24	22	22	22	25	22	24	24
Women	84	85	86	85	86	88	88	88	89	91
Vocational education	25	28	29	31	32	30	29	31	27	28
of which: higher comm. ex.	8	8	7	7	8	7	7	8	7	7
Higher education	59	57	57	54	54	57	58	56	62	63
Short-cycle	10	10	5	4	4	4	4	3	5	7
Medium-cycle	34	33	36	38	37	40	40	40	43	42
Long-cycle	15	15	16	12	12	14	15	14	14	14

Source: Danish Ministry of Education (1994), *Danish Youth Education, Problems and Achievements*.

The pupils are also entitled to State support and most municipal councils offer additional support depending on the income of the parents. In general the parents pay 33-50 per cent for their child's education, board and lodging. In 1992, 223 schools had 17 000 pupils.

Production schools

As a part of the provisions against youth unemployment the municipalities and counties may establish production schools as private, self-governing institutions with a governing board comprising representatives of the founding municipal or county council and of the local labour market's organisations.

These schools offer young people, who have finished compulsory education without having obtained connection with the labour market or completed a vocational education, combined education- and production-programmes. The education must be both practical and theoretical. The theoretical part of the education must be of considerable extent and to the greatest possible extent integrated with the practical work. The concept of the production schools has much in common with that of those continuation schools emphasising practical work and has also been inspired by these schools.

Vocational and educational guidance must be part of the education, and up to four weeks of work experience at a private enterprise or a public institution can form part of the education.

The pupils can attend the school up to one year, and if they are not entitled to draw unemployment benefit they are paid a daily allowance during their stay.

The schools may sell their products on terms not creating unfair competition. The sales income will contribute to the running of the school. The local labour market board ensures that these activities are run in agreement with the local labour market organisations. The establishment and current expenses of a production school — not covered by State subsidies and sales income — are paid by the founding municipality/county.

In 1992, 120 production schools were established and approximately 9 000 pupils attended the schools. The total expenses of the municipalities and counties amounted to 160 million DKr, while the State subsidies amounted to 62 million DKr.

The municipal voluntary Youth School

The municipalities are by act bound to run youth schools for the 14-18-year-olds residents in the municipality.

The Youth School has to give young people the possibility to consolidate and improve their knowledge, help them to understand and qualify themselves for social life and contribute to a richer content of their lives.

The objective of the Youth School is manifold and so is its clientele. Most of the pupils also attend the upper forms of the municipal school, an upper secondary school or vocational education and follow late in the afternoon or in the evening subjects at the Youth School, which they are not able to follow at their main educational institution, *i.e.* mostly leisure-time type of subjects (electronics, word-processing, ceramics, cooking, radio construction, design, etc.). Some take the opportunity to improve their knowledge and proficiency in subjects where they have done poorly during their compulsory education and prepare themselves once more for the final examinations of the *Folkeskole*; some prefer to spend the last two years of compulsory education at the Youth School because the more free concept of the Youth School and a change of environment suit them better, and others want to continue the special education they have received at the municipal school.

Full-time education at a Youth School must on the one hand come up to the normal requirements of the *Folkeskole* and give the pupils the same possibilities for a versatile development and acquisition of knowledge as if they had attended a *Folkeskole*. On the other hand full-time education at a Youth School is not bound by the regulations of the *Folkeskole* on division in forms, sequence of subjects, syllabus, division into lessons, etc.

The Municipal Council may finally also decide that the Youth School shall comprise club and other leisure time activities.

In 1992, 175 000 pupils (approximately 60 per cent of the 14 to 18 age group) attended the Youth School. The Youth School expenses are all paid by the municipalities and amounted in 1992 to 615 million DKr.

Chapter 5

PROBLEMS AND CHALLENGES

The Drop-out Problem of Youth Education

The drop-out rates of the education system is a matter of great concern. Table 13, which is based upon the individual pupil/student statistics, shows the percentage of young people who continue their education or drop out at the different levels of education.

On one side, it seems satisfactory that only 7 per cent drop out after the end of compulsory education, but it is, however, unsatisfactory that 20 per cent of the 93 per cent, who have continued their education in a vocational or an upper secondary education programme, drop out without changing to an other programme.

The drop-out rates are highest in the technical schools' programmes — twice the number in commercial schools — in Higher Preparatory Examination courses (HF) and in courses for the general upper secondary examination (*Studentereksamen*).

In order to reduce the high drop-out of the technical schools 20 schools have embarked upon an experiment together with local municipal schools. The instruction in 40 classes of the 10th form of the *Folkeskole* is integrated with the first school period of 10 technical schools in order to facilitate the transition from general to vocational education.

Evaluations of the experiment indicate that this extended "bridge building" process between the *Folkeskole* and technical schools has made the pupils stay in the education system to a greater extent. They have been far more motivated than pupils traditionally are during the first parts of their technical school career; and the drop-out rate of the test classes has been lower (3 per cent) than elsewhere in youth education.

The experiment continued in 1994, and efforts are made to let "bridge building" become and ordinary educational instrument.

As far as the drop-out problem in Higher Preparatory Examination courses (HF) is concerned the conditions of the HF-courses are under consideration in order to find ways and means to reduce the present drop-out rate of 24 per cent. The situation in courses for the *Studentereksamen* where the drop-out rate is 50 per cent is more difficult to cope with, as many of the students follow evening courses while at the same time having a full-time or a part-time job.

Table 13. **Expected total educational profile of a year group distributed according to whether they get a vocationally qualifying education, by sex, 1981/82 - 1990/91**

	81/82	82/83	83/84	84/85	85/86	86/87	87/88	88/89	89/90	90/91
					per cent					
Total	100	100	100	100	100	100	100	100	100	100
Vocationally qual. educ.	65	65	66	67	69	70	70	68	68	70
Vocational education	40	40	42	45	46	45	43	40	38	39
Higher education	25	25	23	23	23	25	27	28	30	31
Short-cycle	5	5	4	4	4	5	5	5	6	6
Medium-cycle	15	15	13	13	14	14	15	16	16	17
Long-cycle	6	6	5	5	5	7	7	8	8	8
Non-voc. qual. educ.	35	35	35	33	31	30	30	33	32	30
Basic school	12	1	11	10	9	8	8	7	7	6
General upper sec. educ.*	5	5	5	5	5	4	4	4	4	4
Uncompl. voc. educ.	13	14	13	13	12	12	12	16	15	14
Uncompl. higher educ.	6	6	6	6	5	6	6	6	7	6
Short-cycle	1	1	0	0	0	0	0	0	1	1
Medium-cycle	3	3	4	4	4	4	4	4	4	4
Long-cycle	2	2	2	2	2	2	2	2	2	2
Boys	100	100	100	100	100	100	100	100	100	100
Vocationally qual. educ.	67	66	66	68	70	70	68	64	65	65
Non-voc. qual. educ.	33	34	34	32	30	31	32	36	35	35
Girls	100	100	100	100	100	100	100	100	100	100
Vocationally qual. educ.	63	64	65	67	69	71	72	72	71	73
Non-voc. qual. educ.	37	36	35	34	31	29	28	29	29	27

* Of which 2/3 are qualified for admiss on int o higher education.

Source: Danish Ministry of Education (1994), *Danish Youth Education, Problems and Achievements*.

The Act on Vocational Basic Course — EGU

The Social Commission appointed by the Minister of Social Affairs has discussed the drop-out problem in a social context and found that there is a need for a course which can create a coherent but flexible transition to the labour market for the less academically oriented pupils. The Social Commission therefore suggested a vocational basic course ("EGU", the Danish abbreviation for *Erhvervsmæssig Grunduddannelse*). The Minister of Education and the *Folketing* accepted the suggestion and the Act on EGU came into force on 1 August 1993.

An EGU course is to take two years. The course consists mainly in practical training — only 20 to 40 weeks have been set aside for theoretical education. The theoretical education is to take place at already approved educational institutions.

The practical training is mainly to take place in private and public enterprises but may also take place in the form of practical instruction, for instance at a production school or a workshop school at a vocational school.

It is the aim of the education and training to give the young person qualifications which may lead both to further studies in a vocationally qualifying course of education and to create the basis for employment in the labour market.

It is the municipality, where the young person lives, which — in co-operation with the local educational institutions — is responsible when it comes to offering EGU-courses to young people.

The Action Plan "Education for All"

In order to come to grips with the drop-out problems of youth education the Minister of Education in May 1993 appointed a committee which came up with proposals suited to diminish the drop-out rate significantly.

In November 1993 the committee published a report "Education for All" which calls attention to a number of actions to be taken in order to minimize the drop-out rate of youth education. The Minister of Education accepted the report and presented it shortly afterwards to the *Folketing* who gave it a favourable reception.

As a superior target of the Action Plan the committee formulated the following guidelines:

— The pupils should be brought into focus.
— All young people should be challenged.
— All types of youth education should develop the personality and creativity of the pupils.
— The youth education system should make individual educational sequences possible.
— The development of school leaders and teachers should be stimulated through experiments and development projects at the schools.

The government is in the process of implementing the various initiatives. The target is before the turn of the century to raise the present proportion of youngsters who carry through a general or vocational upper secondary training course from approximately 75 per cent to 90-95 per cent.

Action 1. Watch the pupils in order to make them settle down and not to drop out

In Autumn 1993 the Minister of Education made an appeal to all youth education institutions asking them to make a special effort to reduce the drop-out. The campaign continued throughout 1994.

In order to limit the risk of final drop-outs it is crucial to step in with renewed educational guidance immediately after the pupil's drop-out. It is therefore obligatory for the schools to report quickly to the municipal youth guidance service when a pupil has interrupted or is about to interrupt his or her education.

Action 2. The safety net

All young people who are about to leave the *Folkeskole* and/or to begin some sort of youth education should be guided and advised, partly to make them understand the importance of a continued education, partly to give them the knowledge and insight necessary to make a relevant choice of an education which they both can and want to go through with.

Certain groups of young people especially at risk need a closer and more individually supporting guidance taking the young person's total life situation — including the family relations — into consideration. Guidance should thus form a safety net for the young people. It is therefore of decisive importance that an effective interlocking of the municipal youth guidance and the guidance of the *Folkeskole* and the youth education institutions is created.

Action 3. Promotion of the inclination to continued education

The disinclination to go to school is often the reason why some young people do not continue their education after having finished their compulsory education. These young people have *inter alia* lost their inclination to go to school because the literary demands and the traditional class teaching are not in accordance with their means and interests. In the future the *Folkeskole* must try to prevent this disinclination by paying attention to these pupils' own wishes and potentialities. This may *inter alia* be realised by offering 8th to 10th grade pupils alternative educational sequences where the practical and theoretical content is combined.

Action 4. Bridge building

The passage from the *Folkeskole* to youth education will be improved in order to give the pupils possibilities to build bridges according to their own needs combining education and guidance sequences of up to one year's duration. The sequences shall cross the borders between existing offers of education and give the young people time to mature and make their choice of a continued youth education clear.

Action 5. Free youth education

A road will be opened for young people wanting to organise their own education, mainly based upon popular enlightenment offers. This is a recognition of the extensive learning activity which young people choose outside the formal system of youth education. Popular enlightenment institutions wanting to participate in this action must guarantee the quality of the different parts of the education and their coherence through individual plans of education of normally two years' duration for each pupil.

Action 6. Reform of the courses for Higher Commercial Examination (HHX), Higher Technical Examination (HTX) and Higher Preparatory Examination (HF)

The coherence between vocational upper-secondary education (HHX and HTX) and vocational education has turned out to be insufficient, as the present first school year, which is common for both the future HHX and HTX-students and those who want a vocational education and training course of the "sandwich" type, does not satisfy the needs of the two groups.

A committee has therefore be appointed to consider the extension of the HHX courses from two to three years' duration with access directly from the *Folkeskole*. A reform must, however, imply that a new coherence between the courses and vocational education and training can be established based upon relevant general and vocational elements from both types of education.

There is also a need for experiments with an extension of the course for HF from two to three years' duration including combinations with themes and subjects from neighbouring types of education.

Action 7. Capaciousness in the vocational education system

The Council on Vocational Education and the Trade Committees have taken the initiative to adjust the vocational education system and to develop its quality on the basis of experiences gained after the launching of the 1991 reform. The efforts are concentrated on:

— the economy;
— extended experimental activity;
— co-ordination of HHX and HTX with vocational education and training;
— clarification of the placing of the basic subjects;
— the structure of the first school period.

The demands on the content and form of the vocational education system, which apply to the majority of young people should be:

- capaciousness in a system with a more differentiated fan of educational possibilities;
- strengthening of the trade identity from the very beginning of the education and training;
- the final trade level;
- creation of a high level of motivation among the pupils;
- promotion of a gradual personal development.

Action 8. New educational programmes for growth areas

New areas of employment and new methods of work make it necessary to adapt the supply of vocationally oriented programmes in order to avoid "bottle necks" on the labour market. It is especially important to establish new programmes in fields like tourism and environmental protection, where increased employment possibilities are expected. One should also be observant of young peoples' endeavours to create themselves a platform with activities, which hitherto have not been based on a formal education programme.

Within the framework of recognition and financing under the new Act on Vocational Basic Courses (EGU), local experiments with the development of new programmes across existing school boundaries could also contribute to the breaking of new ground and to the covering of temporary needs.

Action 9. Efforts for the benefit of late developed young people

Based upon a report from the Council for Pedagogical Development Work for Late Developed Young People the efforts for the benefit of this group will be continued on a wide front.

The free boarding schools (continuation schools) will be granted means for the establishment of the frames necessary for the teaching of the late developed, *inter alia* buildings and equipment for workshops. Courses and exchange of experiences will be arranged for teachers especially occupied with teaching of the late developed. The Act on Free Boarding Schools (continuation schools) will be amended with an extension of the access to State subsidies for special education to all free boarding schools and all pupils with special needs.

A new order on the municipal youth guidance will ensure that this guidance will take over, when the schools release their hold of the late developed young people. Guidance, supervision and long-term, up-to-date education plans for the individual young person are conditions of a successful effort.

The Minister of Education will initiate an interministerial co-operation on a joint effort with regard to late developed and other groups of functionally impeded young people.

The gross expenses of the action plan are estimated to be approximately 800 million DKr (100 million ECU) per year, distributed on:

— Reduced drop-out rate:	approximately 300 million DKr
— New or extended programmes:	approximately 400 million DKr
— Increased "taximeter" grants in connection with the reinforced bridge building and a HHX/HTX reform:	approximately 100 million DKr

The Minister of Education will initiate a research programme "Education for All". The intention is to improve the basis of knowledge for the further development of youth education according to the needs of young people.

Adult Education

The fast technological development, the growing internationalisation and competition, not least in the European internal market, and the high rate of unemployment call for a vigorous extension of educational possibilities for adults. It is thus significant that the labour market agreements in an increasing degree also comprise conditions on employers' contribution to continued education of the employees.

Labour Market Education (AMU) will still play an important role offering retraining and special courses for unskilled workers and continued education for skilled workers, but the Act on Open Education actually opens nearly all vocational and higher education programmes up for all adults in need of new qualifications and skills. This means new challenges for the vocational schools and the institutions of higher education. On the one hand they will have to accept and give credit for qualifications already obtained by the adult students in an often untraditional way. On the other hand they will have to adapt their instruction to the fact that the adult students will be highly motivated and be in possession of years of working life experience. Finally they will have to develop distant learning systems based upon modern electronic technology.

Credit Transfer

The Act on Open Education, the fact that a growing number of young students will have taken courses abroad and the need of the labour market for people with new and untraditional combinations of courses and subjects have created a need for the introduction of a credit transfer system similar to — or at least compatible with — the British Credit Accumulation and Transfer Schemes and Assessment of Prior Experiential Learning and the EU pilot project European Community Course Credit Transfer System (ECTS).

Part Two

EXAMINERS' REPORT

Chapter 1

INTRODUCTION

Denmark is not new to education reviews. The last one was carried out between 1977 and 1979, and was published in 1980. That review coincided with the then Danish Central Council for Education's comprehensive survey of the Danish education system commissioned by the Minister of Education. The final report of the Central Council, entitled "U 90", did not, for various reasons, become the basis for the planning and development of education policy in Denmark that had been hoped for.

Since that comprehensive country review, there has been active Danish involvement in a number of OECD activities, including, among others, the review of *Adolescents and Comprehensive Schooling*, published in 1987; *The Changing Role of Vocational and Technical Education and Training*; *Overcoming disadvantage and Improving Access to Education and Training*; *The Condition of teaching*, and *Higher Education and Employment*.

The current review was undertaken in response to a formal request to the OECD by the Danish Authorities in May 1991. The then Minister of Education indicated that the main focus of the Review should be youth education, particularly vocational education and training, and that the quality and management of the system should be an important transversal theme.

Between the setting of that remit, and the commencement of the Review, there was a change of government in Denmark. The new Administration and the Minister of Education indicated that the review should continue, as agreed, but that it should also address the issues of student drop-out and failure to gain vocationally useful qualification.

The Background Report, as is usual, has been prepared by the National Authorities, although its shape and content were discussed with the Secretariat, and with the Examiners during their preliminary visits to discuss the review, the Background Report, and the shape and nature of the Examiners' programme.

Denmark is an old kingdom that has retained a remarkable degree of cultural homogeneity over the many years of its existence. Historically, and now, it is both a bridge between Continental and Northern Europe, and a distinctive Nordic State. It is a country of individualistic, non-conformists who are proud to be Danes, but are ambiguous about their relationships with the State, or other large systems of government and administration, as witnessed by the events surrounding recent referenda on the ratification of the Maastricht Treaty.

That ambivalence is also reflected in the national electoral arrangements that have ensured that no single party of government has ever had an overall majority. It is manifested, too, in the differentiation of governance between national, county, and municipal authorities, and most pervasively in Denmark's long tradition of seeking consensus and conciliation in tackling issues in politics, industrial relations, and in communal and personal situations. In part, at least, that mix of individual freedom and consensual politics, has contributed to the general liberality and openness of Danish society, and the wide acceptance of welfare State politics.

Like most countries with few raw materials, Denmark is dependent upon a thriving export trade to finance its imports of raw materials, and maintain a healthy balance of payments. Up to the 1960s it managed to do just that and established, and got used to, a high standard of living. However, through the 1970s and 1980s the balance of payments moved into deficit, and, in common with the rest of Europe in the 1990s it was in recession. Despite that, and an unemployment rate higher than the OECD average, a youth unemployment rate higher than that for the workforce as a whole, a demography leading to a sharp decrease in the proportion of economically active and a large increase in the elderly and economically inactive, Denmark continues to provide generous, and, expensive public services, and its people to expect a high standard of living.

The recession is not confined to Denmark, but in 1993 between 320 and 350 thousand Danes were looking for work, and only a small improvement was forecast in 1994. Furthermore, in common with other developed countries, not all the unemployment is due to recession. Some of it is structural. Given those economic realities, and its lack of natural resources, Denmark is highly dependent upon the skills, qualifications, inventiveness, and entrepreneurship of its people. That dependency is, in part, reflected in Denmark's expenditure on education. As a percentage of total public expenditure it is slightly lower than the OECD average. Compared to GDP, Denmark corresponds to the OECD mean, just behind Canada, the United States, Finland and Sweden.

As is to be expected, the characteristics of the Danish education system reflect those of the wider society. It is generous, inclusive, complex, expensive, and relatively leisurely in pace. Its governance and financial structures are mainly a result of history, and of a long-established distribution of political power and responsibility. The three-tier system (the State, counties, municipalities) is firmly cemented, and seems beyond the reach of any single reforming agency. Philosophically, Denmark's rural beginnings, its long involvement in European academicism and scholarship, and its reputation for high quality products and services, influence its education service. The anti-intellectualism of the "Man from the Plough", the individual freedom of choice of N.F.S. Grundtvig, and the scholarly traditions of central European, are all alive and well today in Danish educational thought, organisation and practice.

As with all countries, Denmark has no choice about the palimpsestic pattern of people, events, politics, ideas, beliefs, geography and climate that are its unique history and which have influenced and formed its culture. Nor has it any other choice than to build on all of that, warts and all, in addressing current problems. We have tried to bear that important truth in mind during our visits, meetings, conversations, and in coming to our conclusions.

We are most grateful to the Danish Authorities for the open, efficient, friendly, and cheerful ways in which they responded to our requests for data, and organised the extensive, and demanding programme of visits and meetings across the country that we requested.

The observations made during those visits, and meetings are the main basis of our report. However, we would not have been able to make effective use of the visits without the aid of the very thorough Background Report, additional, specific documentation, and the personal assistance and guidance provided so willingly and expeditiously by our Danish hosts. All that enabled us, during our visits, to concentrate on the particular, while not losing sight of the general context in which it was set. In addition, it allowed us, in this Examiners' Report, to avoid lengthy description and repeating factual details, while concentrating on the particular features and issues arising from our examination of Danish youth education and training that, in our judgement, seem to call for critical comment and discussion.

Chapter 2

REMIT AND ISSUES

Our remit and approach were directed by the policies and developments in education of the Danish government. The initial remit for this Review was to examine and report on youth education (16-19), with especial attention to the effectiveness of the 1992 reforms to vocational education, and, transversally, on quality and standards.

During discussions between the Danish authorities and the Examiners, it was agreed that the examination of youth education should be set in the context of what surrounds and influences it in Denmark and internationally.

Since that original remit was set there have been radical changes in the economic health and wealth of nations, and a change of government in Denmark. On the broader front, the whole of Europe is in recession. Some twenty million people are unemployed, and a third of those are under 25 years of age. Furthermore, the growing evidence of structural changes in employment, unevenly affecting the young, poorly educated, untrained, unqualified, and unskilled, raises fears about an increasingly polarised society in which those without work are marginalised. Denmark is not immune to those economic and social ills.

The present government is concerned to minimise youth unemployment. While that must involve more than just education, the government is seeking ways to ensure that all young people are offered education, or work experience, and complete a vocationally relevant education. That calls into question the efficiency and effectiveness of the education service, in which the extraordinarily high figure of 94 per cent of the age cohort enters upper secondary education and training, but only 66 per cent enters the labour market with vocational qualifications. Thus, youth unemployment and drop-out from education and training were added to our remit.

In fulfilling that remit we addressed the issues of the economy, efficiency and effectiveness of youth education; steering the system by frameworks and targets, as distinct from detailed prescription and legislation; institutional autonomy; enterprise, co-operation and competition, and new and future directions and developments in education policy and practice.

To address those issues within our remit, we organised our report into the following sections and themes: employment and the labour market; the distribution of policy and financial authority; quality and standards; drop-out; youth education; and before and after (the *Folkeskole* and higher education).

Chapter 3

TRANSVERSAL THEMES

Employment and the Labour Market

The assumptions about long-term developments in employment among OECD countries seemed to apply to Denmark, in that they were borne out by the substance of our discussions with employers, workers, and their associations, and with representatives from the manufacturing and service sectors; college principals, teachers and students. Those assumptions can be summarised as follows:

i) unskilled people face fewer and fewer employment opportunities as qualification levels and requirements are rising;

ii) an increasing number of jobs requires a sound, broad-based, general education that will increasingly be expected to include information technology (IT), and foreign language competence. Vocational and general education will not be alternatives, but will be regarded as necessarily complementary;

iii) personal and social competences, skills and self-confidence are emerging as increasingly important requirements and qualifications, as employment and employers place more emphasis on the need for self-motivating, autonomous workers characterised by versatility and flexibility;

iv) the desirable balance between practice and theory, and between general, academic and specific, vocational education and training in routes to vocational qualification, and employment is uncertain.

Future gazing, and prediction are not exact sciences. They are risky, but necessary activities, especially for those charged with developing economic and social policy. Employment and labour market projections are no exception, but there appears to be some consensus that in the post-industrial, or service economy, the labour market will be divided into distinctive sectors characterised by large variations in productivity, and in the added-value of different work.

The demand for skilled labour and special competences will continue, and probably increase with the advancement of technology in a number of areas, such as marketing, information, financial services, and in highly specialised manufacturing such as medicine, and environmental protection. In traditional manufacturing intensive competition will reduce the size of the manufacturing base in most countries; technological change will cut manpower demands, and economy, efficiency and quality imperatives will contribute to the demand for workers to be better educated in general, and to have higher skill levels.

The service industries do not offer a problem-free alternative to a declining manufacturing base. They have also run into trouble and are experiencing much slower growth. There is persistent, high unemployment in some. Some of that is due to recession and the consequential fall in demand, but there are also structural changes that, at one and the same time, reduce the numbers employed and raise the education and skills demands on those who are in work. Routine jobs will continue to be replaced by automation and "self-service" in the service industries.

That is particularly true of the high value-added services such as banking and financial services more generally. The demand for the lower value-added services will become increasingly price-sensitive, or they will disappear completely. Consequently, for those who, for whatever reasons, do not qualify for high value-added employment, the only alternatives will be low, or even reductions in pay, or to stay outside the labour market.

Solutions to these problems are hard to find, and politically difficult to carry through to implementation. Within the labour market many see solutions in a larger differentiation in wages. That is not easy to achieve anywhere, but would be especially difficult in Denmark with its long traditions of consensus in these matters, and its high level of unionisation. In education and training the call, especially in developed countries, is for an increase in, and a more effective focusing of, the skills in the labour force. That is often allied with raising the general education level of those in, and entering, the labour market.

A better educated and skilled work-force makes sense, of course, especially when set alongside the requirements of high value-added jobs. But, if the supply of such jobs is less than the demand for them, money and time might be spent without reasonable return. Perhaps more damaging, in the longer term, is the possibility that mismatches between qualifications offered and those required might leave a sizeable proportion of better educated and more highly skilled young people with its expectations and prospects unfulfilled.

Of course neither society, the economy, nor the labour market is static. The demographic downturn will bring some counter-balance to the loss, and slower-growth of available jobs in some areas of employment. The emergence of new occupational activities will cause the development and growth of new, or newly devised, training courses. Those developments will bring a degree of dynamism and vitality to aspects of the economy, if those setting the policy directions for education and training are able to do so in ways that enable the system to be pro-active, flexible and speedy in responding to emerging international, national, regional, local employment needs. In addition, policy needs to ensure that pressing economic realities do not obscure that further education and training have not only to qualify for employment, but should promote and further personal development, and prepare young people for adult, social life generally.

Upward drift affecting education qualification and certification, does not only arise from seeking to meet genuine increases in the requirements of further and higher education and training and the labour market. Shortfalls in the supply of high value-added jobs, and/or, of employment generally, can cause employers to select those applicants with the highest levels of educational achievement as a filter to employ the "brightest" applicants, whether or not the requirements of the work in question need entrants at those levels of general educational achievement.

Each and all these factors are present in Denmark. Employers and educators are working together to raise skills levels in, and introduce new competences to vocational education and training courses. Upper secondary and higher education are increasing the proportions of young people staying in full-time education. On the other hand, only some two thirds of young people entering the labour market do so with a vocational qualification.

Employers, given the choice, which many of them now have, are acting incrementally to ensure that they employ the academically brightest applicants. They do that in a variety of ways, but most usually by recruiting, wherever possible, from academically more demanding forms of education and training, such as higher, general upper secondary, and technical and commercial education. That appears to be at the expense of applicants with more specific vocational qualifications. It also appears to be on the increase, possibly because, not only are employers encouraging an upward drift of qualifications, some now believe it cheaper to take the best leavers from upper secondary and give them a short training course, rather than using a complete initial education and training course. In addition, young people, in increasing numbers, are choosing to follow more general, upper secondary courses rather than more specifically vocational routes into employment. Some seem to be doing that because of the greater flexibility, and choice that higher levels of educational qualification give them, and because they are aware of the upward drift that is making a high-level of general education a highly marketable "vocational qualification". Others choose the more general route because of the absence of sufficient practical training places leaves them no alternative.

Faced with all that, Denmark, like all similar States, has a limited range of options. First, it is clear that education alone cannot solve such problems. Second, its responses need to be various and varied. For example, it can set about better focusing its vocational education, and increasing the proportion of young people experiencing, and successfully completing it. It can also set out to raise educational achievement at all levels and increase the numbers benefiting from it. Each of those is being tackled and will be commented on in more details later. In short, however, a range of routes is needed after compulsory education leading to broader basic VET, continued general education, key qualifications in theoretical and practical training that, allied with experience in practice, set out to ensure employability, and flexibility. Each route should not only prepare young people for their initial entry to the labour market, but should lay the foundations for recurrent education and training as future demands and opportunities require. More radically, faced with such change and uncertainty, governments might need to work out new and more effective balance between command and market led responses. To pose the question starkly is to ask, in the light of present realities and our best guesses about the future, whether an emphasis on an all-embracing system of education and training, with specific, and required course and qualification links to particular areas of employment, is more, or less, effective than one that put a premium on improving and widening access to a balanced, general education providing worthwhile qualification at several levels, preparing for self employment, encouraging enterprise and entrepreneurship feature, and letting the market settle entry levels and training requirements.

Distribution of Policy and Financial Authority

Policy and financial authority in the Danish education and training system are divided between the State, the countries and the municipalities. At the State level, the Ministry of Finance decides teachers' salaries and conditions of service within its general strategy for salaries as a whole.

Given Denmark's particular history and culture, the division of authority between the State and local regions and communities is understandable. Similarly understandable, given the central interests of the Finance Ministry in the economy of the nation as a whole, is its involvement in determining salaries and conditions of service for large groups of public employees, such as teachers.

Whatever the gains, some of the consequences of those divisions of authority are particularly problematical in hard-times, when coherent and concerted decision-making and action are at a premium. We are all living in such times at present, and Denmark is no exception. Its complex, and generously funded education system seems unbalanced politically and financially, in that national government does not have the means to implement national goals, even that of promoting vocational education and improved preparation of young people for the labour market. Essentially, the government lacks the overall co-ordination necessary for allocating funds and other resources in accordance with national policy. Consequently, despite the national concern about vocational education, the flow of funds in the education service favours the *Gymnasia*, general upper secondary education, and the *Folkeskole*.

The Ministry of education itself seems over-compartmentalised, even in a single area like youth education, where the different sections concerned with general upper secondary, vocational education and training and vocational oriented upper secondary education are very separate from each other. The distance is even greater between youth education, higher education and *Folkeskole* sectors. That makes for difficulty in having planned and regular overviews of the system as a whole, and of some of its inter-related parts. Even the Ministry of Finance's interest in teachers' salaries and conditions of service does not appear to run on into a concern with the consequences of its decisions, nor, more widely, with the economics and functioning of the education system as a whole.

The Ministry of Education is responsible for vocational education, and upper secondary technical and commercial education. It has decided to introduce market disciplines and opportunities into that part of the system by steering it by frameworks and targets, increasing institutional autonomy, and funding it via a "taximeter" system intended to optimise efficiency. That autonomy is severely restricted, in practice, by the Ministry of Education's continued control of the detail of course procedures and practices, and the Ministry of Finance's control of teachers pay and conditions.

The Counties pay for the rest of general upper secondary education in the *Gymnasia*. However, the Ministry of Education controls curricula, examining and quality assurance, which means, in effect, that it controls staffing. The *Gymnasia* are more generously funded than the technical and commercial colleges. That undermines the development of competition for students between the different providers nationally and regionally, and does nothing to raise the status and attractiveness of vocational schools and education when compared with the *Gymnasia* and general upper secondary education.

In effect, as is the Danish way, no single agency is in overall control of any part of youth education. Consequently, the drive for higher economy, efficiency and effectiveness through competition, choice and other market mechanisms is impeded by central government's retention of detailed statutory rules and collectively agreed, highly specific conditions for staff salaries, working hours, and formal competences. That drive is further weakened because it does not apply equally to all sections of the youth education system.

Most important, if the introduction of market mechanisms is a serious intent, is the separation of decisions about spending, from those charged with managing the system and delivering what it has to offer. The Ministry of Finance determines, nationally, the detailed pay and conditions of service of teachers. Yet it carries no responsibility for, nor seems to show much interest in, the consequences of its decisions for institutional autonomy and for managing and providing education efficiently and effectively. The Counties pay the piper in the *Gymnasia*. While the State block grant assists them in doing that it is the Ministry of Education that calls the tune through its control of curricula, assessment and quality assurance, each of which has direct and immediate consequences for the numbers and qualifications of teachers to be employed.

Formulating realistic and politically feasible solutions to these problems will be difficult, and will have to be done within Danish traditions and circumstances. However, if efficiency and effectiveness are to be furthered by judging achievement against clearly agreed and articulated frameworks and targets, those called to account in relation to those targets must be able to influence decisions about inputs and spending that impinge upon their work and responsibilities.

Quality and Standards

Quality and standards in education are important issues of substance at any time. At times of economic stringency and radical change they assume crucial importance. There are a number of specific reasons for that but, in general, both circumstances separately, or in combination, lead to reduction, rationalisation, and/or, a re-ordering of funding, resources, institutions, courses and time. In those circumstances knowing what is good, why it is good, and what is required to maintain and broadcast it, are at a premium in the eyes of politicians, administrators and practitioners.

Denmark is experiencing hard times economically along with the associated pressures on public expenditure, patterns of employment, and education and training. Given those circumstances it is not surprising that its high-cost, high-quality education service should be scrutinised and questioned. Government interest in such a scrutiny is twofold, namely cost effectiveness and value for money.

In common with the many other governments facing similar circumstances and problems, the last Danish government began to move towards steering the system by statutory frameworks and targets, rather than by detailed, central prescription and description of what needed to be done. Moving from central prescription to steering by frameworks and standards is relatively straightforward when devising frameworks for what students are expected to know, understand, master and experience. Putting in place targets and standards against which the performance and achievements of individual students, and those of the system and its component parts can be assessed, is much more difficult.

Historically, discussions about quality and standards in Danish education appear to have emphasised input and process factors, as distinct from outcomes. Along with the highly developed Danish concern with equity, that emphasis has contributed to the undoubted high-quality of human and material resources, accommodation, and supporting services in the education service, and its "cradle-to-grave" comprehensiveness. That is well illustrated by Danish vocational education and training. In international comparisons its overall quality is high in terms of training objectives, methods, facilities and equipment, breadth of training and its relevance to the world of work. Much the same could be said of the *Folkeskole*, the *Gymnasia*, and adult education.

Despite all that, perhaps, in part, because of it, the Danish education service is peculiarly unreflective about its own performance. That is manifested by the tendency to seek quality assurance by "front-loading" the system through detailing what should be taught and examined, by ensuring high quality accommodation, equipment and materials, and a generous supply of highly qualified teachers, while rarely asking about comparative performance within the system. Yet, if education is to be increasingly steered by frameworks and targets, it is the awareness of comparative performance that is the key to raising standards.

That awareness depends upon agreement being reached about the standards by which the education service and its various parts will be called to account. Without standards that are agreed, generally understood, and assessable in manageable and valid ways, steering by frameworks and targets fails utterly. Distinctions between what works and what does not, and between what is cost effective and value for money, and what is not, are not possible.

There is a risk that the standards used are those that can be easily measured, and that teachers will teach to the test, ignoring all else and, thereby, narrow the curriculum experienced by the students. That is a danger. It can be avoided by first determining what students need to know, understand and experience and, when that is agreed, determining the focus and nature of the assessments. If measurable results are not the only criteria of standards, and the tests relate to worthwhile teaching and learning objectives, teaching to the tests is no problem.

Within the Danish education service there appears to be a relationship between the approach to quality control used in any particular subsection of the service, and how it relates to the government. In higher-education, the Centre for the Evaluation of Higher

Education, established in 1992 to initiate regular evaluations of study-programmes, uses peer-group reviews and site visits. The Centre is a governmental body that ensures that quality control remains in the hands of the government, while the general policy with respect to higher education, arising from the new Act of December 1992, appears to be to increase the autonomy of higher education institutions.

In general upper secondary education the government has the major influence on the nature and conduct of quality control. As pointed out earlier in this report, it does so through the curriculum guidelines and examinations. That control has been extended through the introduction of the "Quality Development Project" in which self-evaluation by teachers, and subject and institutional reviews by inspectors are key components in the comprehensive evaluation of individual subjects. The uncertainty about the part the outcomes of those reviews are to play in bringing about improvements seems closely related to the independence of the teachers in such matters.

Quality control in vocational education is mediated through the Council for Vocational Education and the trade committees, which are assumed to monitor study-programmes continuously. However, while the trade committees formulate the general curricular frameworks that can be adapted to local circumstances, the Ministry of Education retains a quite detailed control of examining and target setting.

Overall, there is a deal of confusion to be resolved, and much to be done in relation to quality control in Danish education if it is to become a reflective system, aware of its strengths and weaknesses, and of what needs to be done to bring about improvement. That degree of self-awareness is both the aim and the necessary nature of a service steered by frameworks and targets. Among the essentials requiring clarification are the scope and limitations of institutional autonomy. Presently, the consequences of the Centre's retention of quality control in general upper secondary and in vocational education are that the institutions, especially the *Gymnasia*, see it as a governmental concern having little relevance to them, whereas in the technical and commercial colleges it reduces autonomy, impedes flexibility in course design, and, on occasions, interferes with the frameworks developed by the trade committees.

The availability of empirical evidence about quality and standards is not a problem. In fact, it appears that, unlike most other developed countries, Danish statistics allow individuals to be traced through the whole system and into employment. With proper safeguards, the sensible use of that data could enable the effectiveness and efficiency of education and training to be gauged at various points. In addition, Danish education abounds with alternative provision, such as continuation and production schools, that are aware of what they set out to do and articulate about what they achieve. Gauging whether or not some, or all the alternatives have any important messages for the mainstream, and whether they give value for money, requires some sustained and orderly study in relation to some agreed criteria of effectiveness.

Overall, more money, time and thought need to be devoted to evaluating and comparing results and performance, outcome variables as distinct from input and process variables. Relatively speaking, little money and time are devoted to institutional reviews. In consequence, very few take place. That lack of resources also contributes, in part, to the sparsity and scantiness of follow-up visits. The main challenges are to define standards, get them accepted by all the interested parties, and ensure that they are comparable across all the component parts of youth education. The outcomes and evidence from that increased evaluation effort should establish a baseline picture against, and within which, individual reviews and teachers' own evaluations can be viewed and judged. In short, the Danish education service needs to systematically build-up a solid, understood culture of evaluation by all involved. Only then could the overall effectiveness and the efficiency of the system be gauged, its particular strengths and weaknesses be identified, and the good practice on which improvement depends be broadcast more widely through the system.

Student Drop-out

Student drop-out, and failure to complete education and training and to gain worthwhile qualifications, are multi-faceted concerns. They lead to material and psychological impoverishment in the individuals affected, they represent a serious waste of "human capital", an unaffordable inefficiency, and can become a serious social problem. Excepting the individual consequences, the other concerns about drop-out are heightened, or diminished by their incidence and degree. Consequently, it is important to be clear about defining terms, about the actual incidence of drop-outs, and about how serious the problem is.

The Danish government has as one of its main policy concerns the achievement, before entering the labour market, of full vocational qualification by the whole youth cohort. It is concerned about individual impoverishment, and about the waste and inefficiency drop-out represents. However, it appears much more disturbed by the potential social divisiveness and unrest that might arise, especially if, as seems likely, drop-out from education and training, and the consequential failure to find work disproportionately affect the poor, less-able and disadvantaged.

In one sense the aim the government has set for itself, namely to ensure an all-providing system of education leading to labour-market-usable, vocational qualification for all, ensures the high visibility of drop-out levels, and failure to qualify. However, how serious drop-out is in reality is not at all clear. Apparently a fairly large number of those who drop out must find their way into the labour market, or unemployment in Denmark would be even higher than it is. Given the current labour market situation, and most projections about its future development, it is clear that there are, and will continue to be, problems arising from the supply of jobs, the upward drift of education and skills demand, and the interplay between price and demand. Finding a route through those issues, in seeking to minimise student drop-out, has to be addressed in more general, and economic terms, than the inadequacies of the education service.

For whatever is to be done, to be done well, depends, in part, on a sound analysis of the dimensions of the problem. Definition is not at all straightforward. For example, concern could be centred on the calculation that around 30 per cent of the age group that enters post-compulsory further education leave the system, at whatever level, as "unskilled". To be added to that are the 6 per cent of the age-group that leaves at the end of compulsory schooling; 36 per cent in all.

More narrowly, drop-outs can be defined as those who leave the system without successfully completing upper secondary education. On that basis the drop-out rate is 20 per cent from all forms of upper secondary, plus the 6 per cent who never enter it; 26 per cent in all.

However broadly, or narrowly defined, drop-out mainly occurs at:

i)	the end of compulsory schooling:	6%
ii)	during, or at the end of the first year of vocational education and training:	13%
iii)	non-completion of 2nd/3rd years of vocational education and training:	5%
iv)	non-completion of higher education:	6%

The crucial figures, and the main challenges for policy and action intended to reduce drop-out are the 6 per cent at the end of *Folkeskole*, and the 13 per cent during the first year of vocational education. Consequently the emphasis should be on what is done, and might be improved or changed in the first year of vocational education and the top end of the *Folkeskole* and its relationship with what happens in the vocational schools. Generally speaking the *Folkeskole* should prepare pupils better for what follows. That would not only contribute to reducing drop-out at the end of compulsory schooling, but also drop-out which occurs later in post-compulsory education by better equipping all pupils to make informed choices and to cope more effectively with new demands, both academic and personal.

Those important issues will be returned to later in this report. For now a number of factors influence Danish drop-out levels that need to be addressed by policy makers and practitioners if:

i) the numbers not continuing after *Folkeskole* are to be reduced;
ii) those in first year of vocational education and training are to be helped to stay on;
iii) drop-out in the second and third years of vocational education and training is to be minimised;
iv) drop-out in higher education is to fall.

Each of those factors appears to be differentially influenced by the reluctance in current circumstances of students to enter the labour market, their fears of becoming unemployed, especially in relation to lower-level, vocationally specific qualifications, the upward drift of students' aspirations, and of skills and education demands of the labour-market, and the selection procedures used by higher education institutions.

Chapter 4

YOUTH EDUCATION

Danish youth education is a rich, diversified and complex offering. The mainstream consists of: the *Gymnasium* and the higher preparatory examination course, offering general upper secondary courses; higher commercial and technical courses; vocational training schemes that are school- and apprenticeship-based, and social welfare and health education and training.

Alongside that mainstream provision there are continuation schools, production schools, and municipal youth schools offering supplementary, pre-vocational as well as alternative courses and educational philosophies. In addition new courses have been added recently. Those are, first, the shortened programmes of one-and-a-half to two years' duration, involving more practice and less theory, intended for the less demanding areas of employment such as industry worker, and cafeteria assistants. Second is the new basic vocational course, the EGU. That lasts for two years and is for those who have not started any course since leaving the *Folkeskole*.

Such a highly diversified and generous system seeks to match the heterogeneity of the labour market, and the mix of different interests, abilities and aspirations of young people. There is a price to be paid for that. The system is very complicated; the presence of so many alternatives allows young people to mark time, delay important decisions, and to avoid the disciplines of the work place for long periods of time. Those alternatives, in part, are also a product of the Danish tendency to avoid decisions, and action that might polarise opinion and reaction, and to opt for consensus. The various components of the sector are subject to different government policies, different funding regimes and are accountable to different bodies.

Consequential on all that are the system's complexity, amount of prescriptive details, and its relative inflexibility in responding to rapidly changing circumstances.

Across the range of youth education there are a number of fairly clear trends emerging. The first is that the length of time spent in all types of schooling is increasing. The second is that, given a choice, students are choosing more general, rather than vocational courses. Consequently, upper secondary education is less and less vocationally qualifying. Currently, about half the age-group chooses upper secondary courses compared with around a third following vocationally specific courses. If this trend continues, and the signs are that it will, it will have the effect of making the upper secondary level more of a foundation, general education stage, and postpone specific vocational qualification until later.

Third is the increasing tendency of the young people to use the system in accordance with their perceptions of how to optimise life and career choices. That is leading to significant movements between the different components of upper secondary education. Those include transfers during, as well as at the end of, courses: 3 per cent of the cohort go onto VET courses from the gymnasium; 7 per cent from the HTX and the HHX. The demarcations between secondary and tertiary education become blurred, as a consequence.

Vocational Education and Training (VET)

In comparison with most other OECD countries VET is highly developed, quantitatively and qualitatively. Some 60 per cent of the age group enter VET; the courses have been modernised and broadened to cover families of occupations, and to provide general, theoretical and practical knowledge and skills through a sound mixture of practice and school education. It is a system in which well-trained, highly motivated, and soundly prepared teachers, working in well equipped schools and training venues, set out to produce skilled, high quality workers able to work autonomously.

VET in Denmark is characterised by the master-craftsman principle based on practice-oriented, on-the-job training, combined with theoretical vocational instruction, and continuing general education in vocational schools. To work satisfactorily, such a system is dependent on:

　i)　the readiness of commerce and industry to undertake training and provide sufficient, suitable training-places;

　ii)　agreement between the parties involved (the State, employers, unions, schools and the wider society), not only to support such a practice-based, "dual" structure, but to agree about how to do so, and to co-operate in maintaining and adapting it to meet new demands of the labour market, and the changing needs of young people.

Despite being such a deeply rooted tradition in Denmark the "dual" or "alternate" system has been under pressure for some thirty years. There are two main reasons for that, namely the growing doubts that the system could satisfy the rising demand for higher levels of general education, theoretical understanding, and transferable skills, and the lack of sufficient training-places, especially, but not only, during periods of recession. The latter problem became even more pressing when, in the 1970s, the introduction of the EFG system made a training place a requirement, and finding them "a duty of the State".

The 1977 reforms mainly addressed the first of those concerns by setting in place a broad "Basic Vocational Year" (EFG) in full-time school form, followed by more vocationally specific practice based on training in the second and third years. In the event labour market realities, and a lack of acceptance in some quarters, led to a critical shortage of training places. In addition, in typically Danish fashion, the traditional apprenticeship system was not abandoned, as had been envisaged. In consequence, two parallel systems of vocational training existed, and the workplace-based apprenticeship remained the more highly regarded by employers with small- or medium-sized companies, and by young people, because they received a salary from the first day.

The reforms of VET implemented in 1991 combined the EFG and the apprenticeship routes to vocational qualification. VET is the sub-sector of youth education where ministerial policy can be most directly influential. The former Minister set out to improve the efficiency and effectiveness of VET by the introduction of steering by statutory frameworks and targets; a direct link between student numbers, time spent to complete studies and funding via the "taximeter" system; competition between institutions; and free choice for well-informed "consumers".

Broadly speaking, the vocational schools appear to like the increased autonomy and flexibility the new arrangements allow them. They are less enthusiastic about: the degree of government commitment to that autonomy; the levels and working of the "taximeter" system; the additional administrative load; and the other powerful player in youth education, namely the *Gymnasium*, which is not subjected to the same financial disciplines and public scrutiny.

There are, however, some clear efficiency gains visible in the vocational schools:

— managerial competence and confidence are increasing;
— heightened sense of responsibility for, and ownership of, what takes place, and what is achieved, among members of governing boards, local trade committees, principals and teachers;
— greater willingness to be innovative within existing programmes and, in a few cases, in devising wholly new programmes;
— belief that, given freedom, with due accountability, to use their funds and organise their work, they could provide better educated and trained manpower for the labour market without substantially increasing costs.

There are also a number of specific problems, such as:

— managerial costs at institutional level tend to rise. That is in part because there is much more that must now be done at that level, rather than at the centre, and also because it is new and people have to gain expertise and experience, and systems must be put in place *ab-initio*;
— there is a growing need for professional, analytic, and administrative support in institutions that might lead to higher costs;
— the uncertainty within which school management must operate is increased, in part, because it comes with the rations in situations of greater autonomy and freedom, but also because the government has stepped back, but without total conviction.

Some of the problems adversely affecting the efficiency of the system arise from the workings of the "taximeter" system. At its present levels it does not appear to have taken sufficient account of the additional planning, administration and organisational loads that fall on the schools. The heads of the VET schools we visited indicated that no leadership/management courses had been offered to them, nor were they encouraged, or obliged to seek such courses out. More generally, if the "taximeter" system comes to be perceived as wholly, or mainly a means of financially squeezing the system, it will come to jeopardise the whole idea of the 1991 reforms, as complaints about declining quality come to dominate the debate. That will be especially so if small schools in more remote areas run into serious trouble, and the political response is to begin to "rig" the whole system by extra-allocations, subsidies and restrictions of student choice.

In fact, the actual system of funding does not appear to be very important. Much more crucial to effective national steering by frameworks and targets is the autonomy of the individual schools. Unless that autonomy is real, in terms of determining spending priorities and organising teaching and learning, the principals and teachers will see little point in continuing to put their efforts into improving the administrative efficiency of their institutions and programmes. Currently, as described earlier in this report, neither the Ministry of Education, nor that of Finance, have followed sufficiently the imperatives of de-regulation.

Essentially, the Education Ministry is still too directly influential in setting out the details of courses procedures and practices, and seems unaware that at times those targets run counter to the objectives formulated by the trade committees. There are also some important gaps, in that trade committees do not as yet exist for some newish areas of VET, including tourism and environmental protection. The Ministry also defines the administrative rules too narrowly, and allows too little flexibility in the allocations of resources between the basic year, and the first and second years of VET courses. A further uncertainty affecting institutional autonomy is that the Ministry sets the "taximeter" rates too low, and changes them too frequently. When it does the latter, it appears to do so on its own terms, and not on the basis of a detailed consultation with those active in the field.

The arrangements about the pay and conditions of teachers, between the Ministry of Finance and the unions impose the most detailed conditions on the institutions. That detail, in itself greatly limits the schools' autonomy, and its flexibility in developing new courses that require teachers to work in different ways and at different times. The fact that the whole of the teachers' pay bill is virtually immovable at institutional level seriously restricts the development of greater freedom and responsibility in determining spending priorities at institutional level. In this context, the Examiners were glad to know that a softening of the very detailed rules concerning the salaries and conditions of service at the vocational schools is on the agenda of the collective bargaining in 1995.

A key to central authorities feeling able to step back from detailed control, to let go of the apron strings, is the existence of agreed and manageable ways of calling the system to account. For that to apply in the Danish VET system the targets need to be better defined, and more effort put into using outcomes, in respect of those agreed targets, to evaluate the performance of the system, and its various components.

The upper secondary courses leading to higher commercial or technical exams (HHX and HTX), provide a sound foundation for further vocational training at a high level, either in higher education or in demanding apprenticeships. About 18 per cent of the cohort take this route, and, even though neither HTX nor HHX provides fully recognised vocational qualification, they do open up entry to higher education. As such they are popular among young people, particularly as their additional vocational qualification makes them attractive alternatives to the *Gymnasium*.

There are, however, a number of problems. The first, and most problematic, is that the lack of training places provided by employers puts in question the validity and viability of a training system in which training in practice is both a cornerstone and a pre-requisite of successful completion. It appears that deficiency is not only a consequence of recession. It has become a structural problem of Danish VET. There are excellent examples of firms that give high-priority to training. In general, however, the manifest readiness, and expectation of employers and their associations to consult with, and be consulted by, government, and to participate in policy formulation, are not matched by a sufficient commitment to investing in training places. There are complex reasons for that state of affairs, and it is not unique to Denmark.

However, if Denmark is intent upon retaining such an all embracing, comprehensive VET system, a pre-requisite is that all areas and aspects of employment recognise the importance of initial, continuing and re-training to their economic health and well-being in an intensely competitive world, by offering sufficient training places. If such wide-ranging provision is not forthcoming from employment, the whole question of "all-providing" VET will need to be radically re-appraised.

In the meantime neither the introduction, in 1990, of school-based practical training programmes, nor the subsidies to employers introduced very recently to encourage the creation of training places, appear to have been very successful. School-based practice is criticised by employers, who have to contribute to its costs, as overly expensive. They do not seem to offer any alternative. Consequently, we are left with the impression that, while school-based training is not the ideal, there is nothing wrong with it, other than its cost. That is a matter for the social partners to sort out, not education. The subsidy appeared to have had only a limited effect in its first year of implementation, and most of the employers with whom we discussed it did not intend to use it.

The most serious problem affecting the effectiveness and efficiency of VET itself is that drop-out in the first year is high. Almost a third of those who enter VET do not end up with a marketable vocational qualification. Together with those not starting VET at all they form a problem group of around a quarter of the age group. The Minister of Education has made helping those young people to undergo further education and training and, thereby, reducing the number without vocational qualifications, a top priority.

Most drop-out occurs during, or at the end of the first year of VET. That basic year is regarded by many of those teaching it as too loaded with theory. That is a consequence of a structural problem affecting the first year. It serves as, not only the first stage of a practice-oriented VET programme, but also as the first stage of the vocationally-oriented, upper secondary course, the HHX and the HTX. It is not at all clear that the first stage can cater effectively, at one and the same time, for laying down the basis of theoretical understanding and skill required by successful continuance in either the HHX, or the HTX, and what is needed to involve the broad mass of ordinary students in an academically more modest and highly practical introduction to VET.

The Ministry is examining the arguments for and against dividing the first year into two strands. It is important, whatever is decided, to seek optimum linkage and permeability between the two strands, and that the options available to students are kept open for as long as possible. The desirability of a close inter-relationship of the two strands should neither obscure, nor obviate, the necessity of ensuring the resources, time and space needed, during the first year, to give individual advice, support and pedagogical help, to disadvantaged and weaker students.

For the majority of first year VET students, the course needs to be more adapted to their personal and educational development. Initially it should be dominated by practical work carefully structured to lead to a growing theoretical understanding as the year progresses. The efficacy of that phasing of practice and theory is born out by the much higher VET completion rates of the young people who begin with a training place in practice. There is no shortage of ideas among teachers and trainers about how such a balance might be achieved in the basic VET year of most programmes. The stumbling block is that "taximeter" rates for the basic year are too low, and the "politics" (vested interests) of each trade programme make it impossible to shift funds from more vocationally specific second and third years, to the basic year. The social partners are crucial to improvements here, as the trades themselves will need to give some ground, if the basic year is to be adequately funded.

The key points appear to be that the first year of VET is trying to serve too many purposes in that it is the lead into apprenticeship linked, occupationally-based courses, as well as being the first step on the way to the three-year upper secondary commercial and technical courses. The first year is overly theoretical for most students, and the occupational courses are massively, adversely affected by the shortage of training places. Consequently, the upper secondary vocational courses are the high-status routes, because they open up a way to higher education, and offer optimum flexibility and choice to students facing an uncertain future. Some vocational schools are already beginning to "stream" the basic year to better prepare some to take the HHX courses in commercial schools. The combined effects of all that are that:

— the growth area as judged by student enrolment, is vocationally-oriented upper secondary;
— the more theoretical nature of those courses dominates the assessment, learning and teaching styles of the first year of VET;
— many students find such approaches inappropriate and fail and/or drop out;
— it militates against the development at local/institutional level, of more adventurous, new courses of initial education and training linking colleges with local employment.

The Examiners noted with interest that, after having read the conclusions of a committee set up to look into these problems, the Minister of Education has presented a bill to the Parliament in January 1994 regarding a change in the vocational upper secondary education courses (HHX and HTX). According to the bill, the vocational upper secondary education courses which are to be organised as 3-year courses with a new link to the vocational education and training courses will give the students the opportunity to change between the courses after the introductory part. This proposal, which entails that in the future it will be possible for the students to organise the vocational education and training courses according to their own aims and in accordance with their own choices and expectations, may also contribute to limiting motivation and drop-out problems within both areas of education. As the bill at the same time provides free access to the vocational upper secondary courses for all qualified students, such a free access to all youth education courses could be guaranteed. In total, the Examiners hope that as expected by the Danish authorities the ongoing evaluation of the 1989 vocational education and training reform, which came into force on 1 January 1991, will uncover good and bad experience and allow for making needed adjustments.

The *Gymnasium*

The *Gymnasia* enjoy the highest status of all upper secondary education, nationally and locally. It is the sector least touched by the kind of reforms pressed on VET by the previous Minister. There are some signs that the *Gymnasia* principals are beginning to be influenced by the notion of competition for students, and that the County authorities, who fund the sector, are beginning to consider how they might press it towards greater efficiency, particularly cost cutting. The Counties are hampered in that by the division of powers between them and the Ministry referred to earlier in this report, namely the Ministry controls and determines curriculum, examining and quality assurance, while the Counties pay the bills.

In respect of questions about quality and standards, the *Gymnasia* seem even less clear than the vocational education and training schools. The only national outcome standard appears to be the upper secondary leaving examination (the *Studentereksamen*) yet, while there are external Examiners, and Ministerial orders describe syllabuses and what is to be tested, it is almost wholly controlled in its conduct and practice by teachers in their individual schools: it is the teachers who are the Examiners and it is they who determine the nature and disposition of the examining. The principals we met claimed that they could explore differences in examination outcomes between different *Gymnasia*, if they wished, and that they could analyse such differences between subjects and teachers in their own schools.

However, the distinct impression we gained was that things were done another way. More typical was the comment of one principal to the effect that "they are good teachers, well qualified, and it is, and should be, the teachers who are the arbiters of quality and of what is effective, important and given priority". There is a deal of truth in that: the professional judgement is highly important and should be influential. There was, however, little recognition or acceptance, among *Gymnasium* teachers, that politicians, parents, employers and students have a genuine claim to have some influence upon the curriculum, and on the standards, competences, skills and understanding that should be encountered, understood and mastered by students.

Beyond the final examination there was little thought given by *Gymnasium* teachers to the use of intermediate standards, or performance indicators, such as the twice termly written papers by students, to gauge and compare across subjects and schools, the effectiveness and efficiency of what they were doing, and whether or not they were on route to agreed goals. Issues on input and process factors dominated all discussions about standards. There was little evidence among teachers of an understanding that part of the price to be paid for being freed from prescriptive, central direction is to clarify about frameworks for courses, and about the performance indicators and the outcome standards needed to gauge whether or not what is supposed to be happening is happening, and is being done effectively and efficiently.

The Counties were conscious of that somewhat embarrassing missing link. Increasingly they were setting targets for "their" *Gymnasia* but had not progressed far down that track, largely because of the lack of feedback about actual activities undertaken by the *Gymnasia* in relation to the general targets. Also, the *Gymnasia* are not subjected to "real" taximeters, or a form of funding that directly links the users to specific costs, income and expenditure disciplines. *Gymnasia* funding is on a time basis and is not only "unreal", in the sense explained above, but is more generous than the VET taximeters.

Being more self-aware and reflective about efficiency and effectiveness is important for the *Gymnasia* not only, nor even mainly, in respect of comparisons with VET schools. Much more pressing is the growing proportion of the age group seeking general upper secondary education. In short the *Gymnasia*, intended originally for the highly academic and scholarly few, around 6 per cent of the age-range, now cater for some 35 per cent, and the pressure for that to increase continues. In such circumstances both maintaining quality, and ensuring that desirable or necessary developments are not impeded, or distorted by outmoded, narrow notions of quality, place a premium on clarity about aims and targets and what is required for optimum efficiency and effectiveness.

Our impression of the *Gymnasia* sub-sector of youth education is that it is undoubtedly a quality sector in terms of inputs and processes, but that it is somewhat complacent and self-satisfied about the degree to which it is cost-effective and gives value for money. In large part that situation stems from the teachers in the sector being too dominant. The *Gymnasia* are clear examples of "professional education organisations" in which the "professionals", the teachers, have the major influence; the *Gymnasium* teacher union is influential nationally and at institutional level, and *Gymnasium* teachers are important and influential members of their local communities. In addition *Gymnasium* teachers were very influential in determining the form and substance of the Upper Secondary Quality Development Project.

That over-riding professional influence will have to be lessened, and other legitimate interests given some opportunity to influence events, if the *Gymnasium* sector is to become a high-quality, mass, upper secondary provider subject to the same economy, efficiency and effectiveness disciplines as the rest of youth education.

Other Youth Education

Leaving aside the usefulness and quality, particularly for special needs, of particular *Efterskole*, *Productionskole* and other small-scale provision in the 16-19 sector, the range and complexity of the provision as a whole raise a general question about whether, or not, the Danish system has a tendency to avoid difficult issues affecting the system, or sub-system, as a whole. Instead of seeking to resolve such issues within the mainstream, it does appear pre-disposed to establish alternative provision. While that might, or might not, be good in itself, it does little to settle mainstream difficulties, and the proliferation of alternatives adds greatly to the complexity and opacity of the system as a whole.

That issue apart, the Examiners did not feel that the *Efterskole*, whatever its intrinsic merits, had much in the way of important messages for this particular review. The *Productionskole* and the Health and Social Skole, on the other hand, certainly had. Those institutions were able, successfully, to motivate and challenge pupils whom the mainstream seemed unable to enthuse or lead through to worthwhile achievement. The general message that they made manifest was that many pupils currently failed by the mainstream could succeed if the mainstream could develop courses with a different balance between practice and theory: in effect moving towards theoretical understanding via practical application and problem solving. In addition both schools demonstrated the advantages gained from teachers working to contracts that were not tied to highly specific, detailed conditions that had to apply, willy-nilly, to all situations.

In particular, the *Productionskoles'* success in motivating pupils through practically-oriented work, poses the question of what would need to change in the mainstream if it were to take those implications on board. In particular how could the work of the *Productionskole* influence the VET basic year, and how might the kind of links with the world of work and enterprise developed in the *Productionskole* inform work experience and courses more generally in VET.

The *Productionskole* we visited raised a very specific issue, namely that it had important lessons to teach about catering effectively for young people and adults with special educational needs (SEN). The school showed us that the mainstream was not for those who, whenever there is a queue for anything, are always at the back of it. Rather, by being distinct and separate, the *Productionskole* was able to create a coherent continuation into education and training for such seriously disturbed and/or handicapped students, by creating its own work and employment.

Chapter 5

BEFORE AND AFTER

The *Folkeskole*

The *Folkeskole* is an important, and unique feature of Danish education, and it is one of which the country is rightly proud. Given the remit of this review, the *Folkeskole* was not a central concern. Consequently, the Examiners did not set out to inspect, or report on compulsory schooling as a whole, or in its own right. Nonetheless, our concern with youth education in general, and with student drop-out in particular, made it necessary to look over the fence at what immediately preceded it.

The present *Folkeskole* Act implies nine years of compulsory education (7-16 years of age). Increasingly pupils are encouraged, or themselves determined, to continue onto a tenth year, many to take the Advanced Leaving Examination. It appears that, currently, around 50 per cent of the age group now take a tenth year course.

An unintended effect of that move is that the new introductory programmes of youth education, such as those at schools for Social and Health Education, are struggling to survive, largely because the numbers of students entering the introductory programmes are falling, as those staying on in the *Folkeskole* for a tenth year increase.

While teachers in the *Gymnasia* and in VET generally welcome the long period of compulsory schooling, they tend to do so on the grounds that, after nine years, or even after ten, the students are not yet ready for what comes next, particularly in VET. That unpreparedness appears to arise, not so much from the length of compulsory schooling, but from the particular philosophy and style of *Folkeskole* education, the lack of understanding of VET, and the absence of physical science and technological competence and confidence among *Folkeskole* teachers, the vast majority of whom are themselves products of the *Gymnasium*.

As to style, one employer, typical of several that we met, put it to us that *Folkeskole* education, and the quality of the teaching within it, had improved immensely in recent times: everything was included, but no pupil needs do anything unless he, or she wanted to; they need not persevere with work. Consequently, pupils who did not receive such guidance and discipline at home, were at risk of not developing the habits and disciplines of work and application that are at a premium in education and training beyond *Folkeskole*.

In short the *Folkeskole* could set out to better prepare its pupils for the next stage, without distorting its historic mission, by adapting style and substance from the seventh year, or by ensuring that the tenth year fulfils that task. Tackling change from the seventh year would involve:

- opening up the curriculum more to the outside world;
- ensuring that pupils learn and work in more independent, autonomous ways, and persevere with tasks;
- extending the understanding of work and workplaces by increasing study visits, and studying, in project form, what makes industry and commerce tick.

The tenth year seems to be growing "like Topsy" with no overall plan, or sense of direction. The Ministry could explore the possibility of bringing some national conformity to the tenth year to ensure that it builds bridges with further education, or, more radically, formally integrates it with the commercial and technical high schools. Whichever route is chosen, if any, the over-riding impression of the Examiners is that the later years of *Folkeskole* ought to provide a better, more consciously directed preparation for what comes next. There are many ways of doing that, but an important criterion should be that the immediate comfort of the pupil should be rather less dominant and decisive than is currently the case.

Higher Education

The Danish higher education system comprises short (1-2 years), medium (3-4 years), and long (5 and more years) higher education programmes. Only some of the medium and all of the long programmes are university level programmes. The strict admission system, occasioned by the scarcity of higher education places, has been loosened in the 1990s as a result of structural reforms to the higher education system that include cut backs. However, restricted admission still applies to a number of programmes.

Since 1993, higher education institutions have been given the possibility of using "free intakes", with the following groupings:

1. disciplines for which the institution is free to decide the size of the intake (technical and natural sciences and technology);
2. disciplines for which the institutions can decide the size of the intake within fixed margins (humanities and social sciences);
3. disciplines for which the Ministry of Education determines capacity (medicine and dentistry).

That implies that institutions themselves determine who they wish to admit to which programmes, within the conditions applying to necessary qualifications, and the number of places they have available. The total number of study places is determined by the government, according to strict quotas, but higher education institutions can vire places across subjects, as they wish.

The general drift of those reforms is to enable higher education institutions to use the study places allocated to them to develop the programmes that are in demand from students. In that way it is hoped that market-like competition for students will be created, and that different institutions will develop distinctive profiles. It is too early to judge whether, or not, that is coming to pass. In addition the new, block grant, higher education funding system, based on the "taximeter" principle, and designed to improve efficiency, rewards lower drop-out rates, and higher pass rates.

Recently a three-year Bachelor's degree has been introduced alongside the existing Master's (Bachelor's plus two years), and Ph.D. (Master's plus three years) degrees. The shorter Bachelors' degrees are intended to lead to increased participation in higher education, and to bring down costs.

The higher education rectors are sceptical about the efficacy and desirability of the recent reforms. They are doubtful about the labour-market appeal of the Bachelor's degrees, and concerned that the emphasis on reducing drop-out will lead to a fall in quality in higher education. Those concerns need to be taken seriously, but the fact remains that Danish higher education suffers from high drop-out rates; it is a long, expensive process that delays entry to the labour-market significantly, and it is not particularly suited, or amenable to the rising demand for higher education of varied and different kinds by increasingly large numbers of young people, employers and government. That massification of higher education, and the undoubted problems about quality that it raises, are not confined to Denmark. All developed nations are experiencing similar demands, and exploring the dilemma of how to expand higher education while maintaining, or even enhancing, standards and quality.

Those issues cannot be resolved by higher education alone. If the Bachelor's degrees, and other shorter, different higher education courses are to become established, the labour market will have to take them seriously. It might be encouraged to do that by being extensively involved with higher education in developing the new courses. The government and the trades unions will need to accept and establish additional, vocationally qualifying points in the education system, that are not priced out of business by being automatically tied into unemployment benefits for the qualified persons who fail to find employment.

On the other hand, higher education in Denmark needs to be much more aware than it is about what is happening in the education service below higher education. There appears to be little communication between higher education and the youth education sector. That is particularly so in relation to VET and to vocationally-oriented upper secondary programmes. Enrolment to higher education from HTX and HHX is very limited, the bulk of entrants, around 80 per cent, come from general upper secondary. Given the quality of many students following vocational upper secondary courses, and that of the courses themselves, that statistic suggests that Danish higher education is far from scraping the bottom of the barrel in terms of the quality of potential students.

Equally important for future development is that Danish higher education needs to react imaginatively, and flexibly to the increased demand for higher education. In doing so it must defend standards and quality, and not lose important babies with the bath water. However, that defence of what lies at the heart of high quality higher education should not be based on narrow, elitist notions of only one route to one kind of academic excellence. If such a "Holy Grail" view of higher education prevails, by definition most people will fail to reach it, the majority will be excluded from even attempting it, and the labour-market will become frustrated by its unworldliness.

Chapter 6

CONCLUSIONS AND RECOMMENDATIONS

Danish youth education is well organised and well provided for. It leads many young people to marketable qualifications and fulfilling education. It is well differentiated to cater for many and varied needs, it seeks comprehensive provision and coverage, and it offers wide ranging opportunities to many people. Despite that, like many other countries, the economic problems and realities that Denmark is facing, have important consequences for education in general, and youth education in particular, because of its direct relationship with the labour market.

Conclusions

Given that reality, a number of important issues arise from our examination of Danish youth education, that are likely to resonate through other Member countries' systems and concerns. Those are as follows:

i) the changing labour market and the nature of the relationship to it of education and training programmes: that is affected by the slow growth in the number of new jobs; the disappearance of non, and semi-skilled jobs; the upward drift of required skills and education; the costs of qualification mismatch and the disappointment of highly qualified unemployed; the social consequences of structural unemployment among the least educated and most disadvantaged;

ii) the distribution of policy and financial authority, and policy co-ordination: there are many actors in the scene, each having different kinds of authority. That allows variety and local decision-making, but it also brings tensions particularly in relation to the co-ordination of action across the system, the determining of priorities for action and funding, and the pursuance of nationally desirable policies;

iii) the nature of vocational education and training (VET): how viable is the "sandwich" system of VET when employment cannot provide sufficient, suitable training places? Is that shortage a feature of temporary recession, or a permanent characteristic of an increasingly competitive labour market? There are indications that some VET programmes are still too detailed, prescriptive and inflexible, and risk being left high and dry by a rapidly changing employment scene. Those programmes need to be broadened, while not losing sight of the need to retain a mix of theory and practice that confers key general, and specific skills intended to maximise employability and flexibility in a fast moving labour market. It might be necessary to develop more general VET programmes with looser links to the labour market, and to use work-simulation and short "internships" rather than work placements. Developing effective and efficient simulated, school-based training programmes must ensure their credibility in the eyes of employers and students and that they are affordable. All of that requires the involvement of education and the social partners, if working, acceptable compromises are to be found;

iv) quality control: the signs are that education and VET systems everywhere are moving towards being steered by means of statutory frameworks and standards rather than by detailed, central prescription. There are a number of reasons for that concerned with efficiency and effectiveness, as well as to do with uncertainty about what will be required in the future. In such circumstances quality becomes increasingly important, to call the system and its various parts to account, to ensure that what is good is retained during periods of retraction, and to ensure that what needs to be developed to improve the system is recognised. The challenge is to establish, and broadly agree, performance indicators, and outcome standards of various kinds by which to judge and compare performance and to then determine which inputs and processes, quantitative, or qualitative, are necessary to high standards.

Finally, a key question that has arisen during this Review is whether, faced with current economic realities, education and training policy should move further towards central direction and control through specific statute, or towards deregulation, allowing greatly increased freedom and autonomy to institutions within broad, statutory national frameworks, and targets. Youth education in Denmark is currently, uneasily positioned between those two stools. As will be the case in most countries, the system will, in the end, be controlled by a particular mix of central prescription and looser steering. Deciding just what that balance is to be is a crucial task for national politicians. Taking whatever soundings they feel necessary, they must decide the parameters of prescription and deregulation, if the other important actors are to operate effectively and efficiently. The Danish government has not yet made clear where it proposes to set that balance to a system that is currently subject to a somewhat confusing, and confused mix of, deregulatory and command messages.

Recommendations

These consequences and issues emerging from the above conclusions are not confined to Danish youth education and training, but, in our opinion, there are a number of matters that need to be addressed by the Danish authorities if the efficiency and effectiveness of youth education in Denmark are to be improved, and drop-out is to be reduced. Our recommendations are as follows:

i) the latter year (years 7 to 10), in the *Folkeskole* ought to better prepare all pupils for the next stage education and training. In particular the *Folkeskole* should lay better foundations for those entering subsequent VET courses, in part by strengthening links between *Folkeskole* and basic VET;

ii) remedial education and special programmes should be developed to support disadvantaged or slow-learning pupils. The programmes should aim to return or to retain students in the mainstream of education and training, and not be seen as alternatives to it;

iii) as a matter of urgency, develop a basic VET year that sets out to build understanding, skill and competence on the basis of a much more practical, problem-solving methodology. Such developments seem much more promising than devising yet more, different courses. The instalment of new training courses parallel to basic VET should be reviewed and co-ordinated. Shorter courses do not seem suited to ensuring the employability of disadvantaged and theoretically weaker students. Crucial to the development of basic VET are an enhanced "taximeter" level for basic VET year, and less national prescription about the nature of the course;

iv) in the continuing absence of sufficient practice places in industry, wholeheartedly set out to develop, and provide school-based work simulation as the acceptable and available alternative. The social partners should be involved in such developments, and should contribute significantly to the costs;

v) make a high degree of institutional autonomy a reality by enabling schools and employers locally to develop new, different kinds of co-operation and initial training courses within a broad national regulatory framework. In addition, by setting out, over time, to reduce the degree of prescription and detail in the national agreement on teachers' pay and conditions of service negotiated by the Ministry of Finance and the unions. That reduction should be such as to enable institutions to match staffing levels and patterns of working to the needs of students, employment, and courses, rather than vice-versa;

vi) establish national working-parties to determine and devise clear outcome measures, and in-course financial and performance indicators by which the effectiveness and efficiency of the system and its component parts can be judged and their strengths and weaknesses identified and used as a basis for action aimed at improvement;

vii) systematically examine effective practice in small-scale provision such as the Production and Health and Social Skoles in order to gauge what can and should be introduced to the mainstream of youth education to enhance its capacity to motivate and retain students. In particular the flexibility and practicality of the courses and their methodologies, and the general nature of teacher contracts should be studied carefully to gauge the desirability and possibility of replication in the mainstream;

viii) continue, systemically, to reduce prescription and regulation in order to optimise creativity and individual enterprise, as well as clear lines of responsibility and accountability at institutional level. In addition, nationally, to work with the social partners to disentangle some of the cat's cradle of overlapping and interwoven agreements and conditions that reduce the capacity of individuals and parts of the system to be pro-active in responding to rapidly moving events, needs and circumstances;

ix) aim, over time, to bring the *Gymnasia* into similar arrangements of institutional autonomy, accountability and funding that apply to VET, and, thereby, put all youth education on an equal footing.

A crucial determinant of youth education policy and practice is the analysis of what is happening to work and the labour market, and what that implies for practice in education and training. None of that is an exact science, but there seems to be wide agreement that, even when recession ends, structural changes will cause there to be fewer jobs, an upward drift in the education and skill levels required of workers, and many non, and semi-skilled jobs will disappear.

MAIN SALES OUTLETS OF OECD PUBLICATIONS
PRINCIPAUX POINTS DE VENTE DES PUBLICATIONS DE L'OCDE

ARGENTINA – ARGENTINE
Carlos Hirsch S.R.L.
Galería Güemes, Florida 165, 4° Piso
1333 Buenos Aires   Tel. (1) 331.1787 y 331.2391
                    Telefax: (1) 331.1787

AUSTRALIA – AUSTRALIE
D.A. Information Services
648 Whitehorse Road, P.O.B 163
Mitcham, Victoria 3132   Tel. (03) 873.4411
                         Telefax: (03) 873.5679

AUSTRIA – AUTRICHE
Gerold & Co.
Graben 31
Wien I   Tel. (0222) 533.50.14
         Telefax: (0222) 512.47.31.29

BELGIUM – BELGIQUE
Jean De Lannoy
Avenue du Roi 202
B-1060 Bruxelles   Tel. (02) 538.51.69/538.08.41
                   Telefax: (02) 538.08.41

CANADA
Renouf Publishing Company Ltd.
1294 Algoma Road
Ottawa, ON K1B 3W8   Tel. (613) 741.4333
                     Telefax: (613) 741.5439
Stores:
61 Sparks Street
Ottawa, ON K1P 5R1   Tel. (613) 238.8985
211 Yonge Street
Toronto, ON M5B 1M4   Tel. (416) 363.3171
                      Telefax: (416)363.59.63
Les Éditions La Liberté Inc.
3020 Chemin Sainte-Foy
Sainte-Foy, PQ G1X 3V6   Tel. (418) 658.3763
                         Telefax: (418) 658.3763

Federal Publications Inc.
165 University Avenue, Suite 701
Toronto, ON M5H 3B8   Tel. (416) 860.1611
                      Telefax: (416) 860.1608

Les Publications Fédérales
1185 Université
Montréal, QC H3B 3A7   Tel. (514) 954.1633
                       Telefax: (514) 954.1635

CHINA – CHINE
China National Publications Import
Export Corporation (CNPIEC)
16 Gongti E. Road, Chaoyang District
P.O. Box 88 or 50
Beijing 100704 PR   Tel. (01) 506.6688
                    Telefax: (01) 506.3101

CHINESE TAIPEI – TAIPEI CHINOIS
Good Faith Worldwide Int'l. Co. Ltd.
9th Floor, No. 118, Sec. 2
Chung Hsiao E. Road
Taipei   Tel. (02) 391.7396/391.7397
         Telefax: (02) 394.9176

CZECH REPUBLIC – RÉPUBLIQUE TCHÈQUE
Artia Pegas Press Ltd
Narodni Trida 25
POB 825
111 21 Praha 1   Tel. 26.65.68
                 Telefax: 26.20.81

DENMARK – DANEMARK
Munksgaard Book and Subscription Service
35, Nørre Søgade, P.O. Box 2148
DK-1016 København K   Tel. (33) 12.85.70
                      Telefax: (33) 12.93.87

EGYPT – ÉGYPTE
Middle East Observer
41 Sherif Street
Cairo   Tel. 392.6919
        Telefax: 360-6804

FINLAND – FINLANDE
Akateeminen Kirjakauppa
Keskuskatu 1, P.O. Box 128
00100 Helsinki
Subscription Services/Agence d'abonnements :
P.O. Box 23
00371 Helsinki   Tel. (358 0) 12141
                 Telefax: (358 0) 121.4450

FRANCE
OECD/OCDE
Mail Orders/Commandes par correspondance:
2, rue André-Pascal
75775 Paris Cedex 16   Tel. (33-1) 45.24.82.00
                       Telefax: (33-1) 49.10.42.76
                       Telex: 640048 OCDE
Orders via Minitel, France only/
Commandes par Minitel, France exclusivement :
36 15 OCDE

OECD Bookshop/Librairie de l'OCDE :
33, rue Octave-Feuillet
75016 Paris   Tel. (33-1) 45.24.81.81
              (33-1) 45.24.81.67

Documentation Française
29, quai Voltaire
75007 Paris   Tel. 40.15.70.00

Gibert Jeune (Droit-Économie)
6, place Saint-Michel
75006 Paris   Tel. 43.25.91.19

Librairie du Commerce International
10, avenue d'Iéna
75016 Paris   Tel. 40.73.34.60

Librairie Dunod
Université Paris-Dauphine
Place du Maréchal de Lattre de Tassigny
75016 Paris   Tel. (1) 44.05.40.13

Librairie Lavoisier
11, rue Lavoisier
75008 Paris   Tel. 42.65.39.95

Librairie L.G.D.J. - Montchrestien
20, rue Soufflot
75005 Paris   Tel. 46.33.89.85

Librairie des Sciences Politiques
30, rue Saint-Guillaume
75007 Paris   Tel. 45.48.36.02

P.U.F.
49, boulevard Saint-Michel
75005 Paris   Tel. 43.25.83.40

Librairie de l'Université
12a, rue Nazareth
13100 Aix-en-Provence   Tel. (16) 42.26.18.08

Documentation Française
165, rue Garibaldi
69003 Lyon   Tel. (16) 78.63.32.23

Librairie Decitre
29, place Bellecour
69002 Lyon   Tel. (16) 72.40.54.54

Librairie Sauramps
Le Triangle
34967 Montpellier Cedex 2   Tel. (16) 67.58.85.15
                            Telefax: (16) 67.58.27.36

GERMANY – ALLEMAGNE
OECD Publications and Information Centre
August-Bebel-Allee 6
D-53175 Bonn   Tel. (0228) 959.120
               Telefax: (0228) 959.12.17

GREECE – GRÈCE
Librairie Kauffmann
Mavrokordatou 9
106 78 Athens   Tel. (01) 32.55.321
                Telefax: (01) 32.30.320

HONG-KONG
Swindon Book Co. Ltd.
Astoria Bldg. 3F
34 Ashley Road, Tsimshatsui
Kowloon, Hong Kong   Tel. 2376.2062
                     Telefax: 2376.0685

HUNGARY – HONGRIE
Euro Info Service
Margitsziget, Európa Ház
1138 Budapest   Tel. (1) 111.62.16
                Telefax: (1) 111.60.61

ICELAND – ISLANDE
Mál Mog Menning
Laugavegi 18, Pósthólf 392
121 Reykjavik   Tel. (1) 552.4240
                Telefax: (1) 562.3523

INDIA – INDE
Oxford Book and Stationery Co.
Scindia House
New Delhi 110001   Tel. (11) 331.5896/5308
                   Telefax: (11) 332.5993
17 Park Street
Calcutta 700016   Tel. 240832

INDONESIA – INDONÉSIE
Pdii-Lipi
P.O. Box 4298
Jakarta 12042   Tel. (21) 573.34.67
                Telefax: (21) 573.34.67

IRELAND – IRLANDE
Government Supplies Agency
Publications Section
4/5 Harcourt Road
Dublin 2   Tel. 661.31.11
           Telefax: 475.27.60

ISRAEL
Praedicta
5 Shatner Street
P.O. Box 34030
Jerusalem 91430   Tel. (2) 52.84.90/1/2
                  Telefax: (2) 52.84.93

R.O.Y. International
P.O. Box 13056
Tel Aviv 61130   Tel. (3) 49.61.08
                 Telefax: (3) 544.60.39

Palestinian Authority/Middle East:
INDEX Information Services
P.O.B. 19502
Jerusalem   Tel. (2) 27.12.19
            Telefax: (2) 27.16.34

ITALY – ITALIE
Libreria Commissionaria Sansoni
Via Duca di Calabria 1/1
50125 Firenze   Tel. (055) 64.54.15
                Telefax: (055) 64.12.57
Via Bartolini 29
20155 Milano   Tel. (02) 36.50.83

Editrice e Libreria Herder
Piazza Montecitorio 120
00186 Roma   Tel. 679.46.28
             Telefax: 678.47.51

Libreria Hoepli
Via Hoepli 5
20121 Milano   Tel. (02) 86.54.46
               Telefax: (02) 805.28.86

Libreria Scientifica
Dott. Lucio de Biasio 'Aeiou'
Via Coronelli, 6
20146 Milano   Tel. (02) 48.95.45.52
               Telefax: (02) 48.95.45.48

JAPAN – JAPON
OECD Publications and Information Centre
Landic Akasaka Building
2-3-4 Akasaka, Minato-ku
Tokyo 107   Tel. (81.3) 3586.2016
            Telefax: (81.3) 3584.7929

KOREA – CORÉE
Kyobo Book Centre Co. Ltd.
P.O. Box 1658, Kwang Hwa Moon
Seoul   Tel. 730.78.91
        Telefax: 735.00.30

MALAYSIA – MALAISIE
University of Malaya Bookshop
University of Malaya
P.O. Box 1127, Jalan Pantai Baru
59700 Kuala Lumpur
Malaysia   Tel. 756.5000/756.5425
   Telefax: 756.3246

MEXICO – MEXIQUE
Revistas y Periodicos Internacionales S.A. de C.V.
Florencia 57 - 1004
Mexico, D.F. 06600   Tel. 207.81.00
   Telefax: 208.39.79

NETHERLANDS – PAYS-BAS
SDU Uitgeverij Plantijnstraat
Externe Fondsen
Postbus 20014
2500 EA's-Gravenhage   Tel. (070) 37.89.880
Voor bestellingen: Telefax: (070) 34.75.778

NEW ZEALAND
NOUVELLE-ZÉLANDE
Legislation Services
P.O. Box 12418
Thorndon, Wellington   Tel. (04) 496.5652
   Telefax: (04) 496.5698

NORWAY – NORVÈGE
Narvesen Info Center – NIC
Bertrand Narvesens vei 2
P.O. Box 6125 Etterstad
0602 Oslo 6   Tel. (022) 57.33.00
   Telefax: (022) 68.19.01

PAKISTAN
Mirza Book Agency
65 Shahrah Quaid-E-Azam
Lahore 54000   Tel. (42) 353.601
   Telefax: (42) 231.730

PHILIPPINE – PHILIPPINES
International Book Center
5th Floor, Filipinas Life Bldg.
Ayala Avenue
Metro Manila   Tel. 81.96.76
   Telex 23312 RHP PH

PORTUGAL
Livraria Portugal
Rua do Carmo 70-74
Apart. 2681
1200 Lisboa   Tel. (01) 347.49.82/5
   Telefax: (01) 347.02.64

SINGAPORE – SINGAPOUR
Gower Asia Pacific Pte Ltd.
Golden Wheel Building
41, Kallang Pudding Road, No. 04-03
Singapore 1334   Tel. 741.5166
   Telefax: 742.9356

SPAIN – ESPAGNE
Mundi-Prensa Libros S.A.
Castelló 37, Apartado 1223
Madrid 28001   Tel. (91) 431.33.99
   Telefax: (91) 575.39.98

Libreria Internacional AEDOS
Consejo de Ciento 391
08009 – Barcelona   Tel. (93) 488.30.09
   Telefax: (93) 487.76.59

Llibreria de la Generalitat
Palau Moja
Rambla dels Estudis, 118
08002 – Barcelona
   (Subscripcions) Tel. (93) 318.80.12
   (Publicacions) Tel. (93) 302.67.23
   Telefax: (93) 412.18.54

SRI LANKA
Centre for Policy Research
c/o Colombo Agencies Ltd.
No. 300-304, Galle Road
Colombo 3   Tel. (1) 574240, 573551-2
   Telefax: (1) 575394, 510711

SWEDEN – SUÈDE
Fritzes Customer Service
S–106 47 Stockholm   Tel. (08) 690.90.90
   Telefax: (08) 20.50.21

Subscription Agency/Agence d'abonnements :
Wennergren-Williams Info AB
P.O. Box 1305
171 25 Solna   Tel. (08) 705.97.50
   Telefax: (08) 27.00.71

SWITZERLAND – SUISSE
Maditec S.A. (Books and Periodicals - Livres
et périodiques)
Chemin des Palettes 4
Case postale 266
1020 Renens VD 1   Tel. (021) 635.08.65
   Telefax: (021) 635.07.80

Librairie Payot S.A.
4, place Pépinet
CP 3212
1002 Lausanne   Tel. (021) 341.33.47
   Telefax: (021) 341.33.45

Librairie Unilivres
6, rue de Candolle
1205 Genève   Tel. (022) 320.26.23
   Telefax: (022) 329.73.18

Subscription Agency/Agence d'abonnements :
Dynapresse Marketing S.A.
38 avenue Vibert
1227 Carouge   Tel. (022) 308.07.89
   Telefax: (022) 308.07.99

See also – Voir aussi :
OECD Publications and Information Centre
August-Bebel-Allee 6
D-53175 Bonn (Germany)   Tel. (0228) 959.120
   Telefax: (0228) 959.12.17

THAILAND – THAÏLANDE
Suksit Siam Co. Ltd.
113, 115 Fuang Nakhon Rd.
Opp. Wat Rajbopith
Bangkok 10200   Tel. (662) 225.9531/2
   Telefax: (662) 222.5188

TURKEY – TURQUIE
Kültür Yayinlari Is-Türk Ltd. Sti.
Atatürk Bulvari No. 191/Kat 13
Kavaklidere/Ankara   Tel. 428.11.40 Ext. 2458
Dolmabahce Cad. No. 29
Besiktas/Istanbul   Tel. 260.71.88
   Telefax: 43482B

UNITED KINGDOM – ROYAUME-UNI
HMSO
Gen. enquiries   Tel. (071) 873 0011
Postal orders only:
P.O. Box 276, London SW8 5DT
Personal Callers HMSO Bookshop
49 High Holborn, London WC1V 6HB
   Telefax: (071) 873 8200
Branches at: Belfast, Birmingham, Bristol,
Edinburgh, Manchester

UNITED STATES – ÉTATS-UNIS
OECD Publications and Information Center
2001 L Street N.W., Suite 650
Washington, D.C. 20036-4910 Tel. (202) 785.6323
   Telefax: (202) 785.0350

VENEZUELA
Libreria del Este
Avda F. Miranda 52, Aptdo. 60337
Edificio Galipán
Caracas 106   Tel. 951.1705/951.2307/951.1297
   Telegram: Libreste Caracas

Subscription to OECD periodicals may also be placed through main subscription agencies.

Les abonnements aux publications périodiques de l'OCDE peuvent être souscrits auprès des principales agences d'abonnement.

Orders and inquiries from countries where Distributors have not yet been appointed should be sent to: OECD Publications Service, 2 rue André-Pascal, 75775 Paris Cedex 16, France.

Les commandes provenant de pays où l'OCDE n'a pas encore désigné de distributeur peuvent être adressées a : OCDE, Service des Publications, 2, rue André-Pascal, 75775 Paris Cedex 16, France.

5-1995

OECD PUBLICATIONS, 2 rue André-Pascal, 75775 PARIS CEDEX 16
PRINTED IN FRANCE
(91 95 08 1) ISBN 92-64-14475-7 - No. 47783 1995